COLLEGE

GCSE LAW CASEBOOK

GCSE LAW CASEBOOK

Third Edition

David Corns BA, PGCE

and

Eric Boucher LLB, PGCE, MCIBSE

BLACKSTONE
PRESS LIMITED

First published in Great Britain 1989 by Blackstone Press Limited, 9-15 Aldine Street, London W12 8AW. Telephone: 0181-740 1173

First edition, 1989
Second edition, 1992
Third edition, 1995

ISBN: 1 85431 464 5

British Library Cataloguing in Publication Data
A CIP cataloguing record for this book is available from the British Library

Cartoons drawn by Anne Lee

Typeset by Montage Studios Limited, Tonbridge, Kent
Printed by Bell & Bain Limited, Glasgow

CONTENTS

For Elizabeth and Vivien

INTRODUCTION

The opportunity has been taken to include some of the more recent important decisions, also some earlier cases following suggestions from users of the *Casebook*.

A small section dealing with European law cases has been included.

Once again, we should like to record our thanks to Alistair, Heather and all at Blackstone Press for their continued help.

INTRODUCTION TO THE FIRST EDITION

A knowledge of relevant cases and how they should be used in answers is essential if a student is to be successful in GCSE Law. Examiners have often commented that many candidates have failed to support their answers by referring to relevant cases and this omission is one of the most common causes of failure to achieve a good grade of pass in the GCSE examination.

This book aims to provide the student with all case requirements by providing in a single, clear and concise text:

(a)   details of many of the cases likely to be needed for GCSE, in a 'case a page' format;

(b)   a commentary on the legal significance of each case;

(c)   comprehensive indexes;

(d)   a guide to the way in which cases should be incorporated into answers.

In limiting this case book to 100 cases there must, inevitably, be some omission of cases which could be useful to GCSE students.

A margin for notes to be added by students is provided at the side of each case.

Although primarily intended for GCSE Law students it is hoped that the clarity of the layout and the straightforward approach will appeal to students commencing the subject at other levels, such as BTEC and GCE 'A' level courses.

We should like to record our thanks to Alistair and all at Blackstone Press for their invaluable help.

CASE REFERENCES

For the benefit of students who have access to a law library and who may wish to read fuller accounts of any case in the law reports, a reference is given under the title of each case.

The reference is set out in the standard form:

Year of case Volume number Report abbreviation Page number

Note that the year of the case is always enclosed in either:

square brackets [   ]   to indicate that the year is needed to find the report, the volume number not being sufficient,

or

round brackets (   )   to indicate that the year is not needed to find the report, the volume number being sufficient.

Some confusion may be experienced with case titles involving appeals to the House of Lords, as prior to 1974 these case titles were reversed on such an appeal. For example: *Smith* v *Jones* would become *Jones* v *Smith* if Jones took an appeal to the House of Lords.

A list of law report abbreviations used in this casebook will be found on p. 10.

LAW REPORT ABBREVIATIONS

AC	Appeal Cases Reports (House of Lords/Privy Council)
All ER	All England Weekly Reports
All ER Rep	All England Reports (Reprints)
App Cas	Appeal Cases Reports (prior to 1891)
B & Ad	Barnwell and Adolphus Law Reports
Bing	Bingham Law Reports
Bing NC	Bingham New Cases
Ch D	Chancery Division of the High Court Reports (prior to 1891)
Ch	Chancery Division of the High Court Reports
Co Rep	Sir Edward Coke Reports
CP	Common Pleas Cases
Cr App Rep	Cohen Criminal Appeal Reports
ECJ	European Court of Justice Reports
EG	Estates Gazette
ER/ER Rep	The 'English Reports' (collected reprints of private reports)
Ex D	Exchequer Division of the High Court Reports (before abolition)
Fam	Family Division of the High Court Reports
H & C	Hurlstone and Coltman Law Reports
Hob	Hobart Law Reports
ICR	Industrial Case Reports
KB	King's Bench of the High Court Reports
LR	Law Reports from 1865 (all courts)
LT	Law Times New Series
QB	Queen's Bench of the High Court Reports
QBD	Queen's Bench of the High Court Reports (prior to 1891)
RTR	Road Traffic Reports
SJ	Solicitors' Journal Reports
WR	Weekly Reporter
WLR	Weekly Law Reports from 1953 (all courts)

TABLE OF CASES

TABLE OF CASES BY TYPE OF LAW

LAW OF CONTRACT

LAW OF TORT

CRIMINAL LAW

EUROPEAN LAW

SEX DISCRIMINATION LAW

ALCOCK v CHIEF CONSTABLE OF SOUTH YORKSHIRE

The Times, 29 November 1991

THE FACTS   Just before the start of a football match at the Hillsborough Stadium, Sheffield, on 15 April 1989 the crowd control by the South Yorkshire police broke down and there was a crush of spectators in one of the stands resulting in 95 deaths and over 400 injuries. The police admitted liability in negligence and Mr Alcock claimed for the nervous shock he had suffered in witnessing, from the other end of the stadium, the accident in which his brother-in-law was killed. Mr Alcock had also identified the body of his brother-in-law after the accident.

At first instance Mr Alcock's claim was upheld but the Court of Appeal allowed an appeal by the Chief Constable so Mr Alcock further appealed to the House of Lords. The House of Lords took the opportunity to consider appeals by nine other claimants for nervous shock arising from either witnessing or watching television pictures of the accident in which they had relatives either killed or injured.

THE DECISION   The House of Lords rejected the appeals by Mr Alcock and all the other nine claimants on the grounds that mere foreseeability that a negligent act resulting in the death of, or injury to, a relation of a plaintiff would cause that plaintiff nervous shock either at the time or soon afterwards was not, of itself, sufficient.

In addition, there was a 'proximity' test to be satisfied. The relationship between the person suffering the nervous shock and the person killed or injured must be one of love and affection. A relationship of love and affection could be presumed to exist only between parents/children, husbands/wives and persons engaged to be married. Also the person suffering the nervous shock must be sufficiently near to the killed or injured person either at the time of the accident or soon afterwards.

Watching television pictures of the stadium accident could not be equated with being within sight or hearing of the accident or its immediate aftermath. Of the claimants actually present in the stadium at the time of the accident (which included Mr Alcock) the relationships with the victims were not within the love and affection category.

ALCOCK v CHIEF CONSTABLE OF
SOUTH YORKSHIRE — *continued*

COMMENTARY In the case of *McLoughlin* v *O'Brian* (p. 114–15) the House of Lords established that if it was foreseeable that negligence by A, causing physical harm to B, could cause nervous shock to C, liability for that nervous shock existed. This decision illustrates that the McLoughlin case may have opened the door too wide to nervous shock claims so their Lordships have developed their earlier decision so as to limit its application. The rejection of claims for nervous shock from watching television pictures of the accident is based on the fact that no one could be identified from the pictures.

ALLCARD v SKINNER

(1887) 36 Ch D 145

THE FACTS   The plaintiff entered a protestant Order known as 'The Sisters of the Poor'. Her vow of poverty required her to surrender her worldly possessions — some £7,000 — to the Order. Six years after leaving she sued for the return of the £1,671 which had not been spent by the Order, claiming that it had been obtained as a result of undue influence of the Lady Superior (the defendant).

THE DECISION   The plaintiff had no opportunity of seeking external advice and so should have been able to recover the remaining money on the basis of undue influence, but her claim failed due to her six-year delay in bringing the action.

COMMENTARY   Undue influence is a subtle form of pressure exerted by one party to the contract on the other such that the judgment of the party influenced is not freely exercised and their consent not freely given. It arises when the relationship of the parties to an agreement is not based on equality.

Where undue influence exists the contract is voidable at the option of the party influenced.

In the following relationships of trust there is a presumption of undue influence. This means that to escape liability the defendant must rebut the presumption, i.e., satisfy the court that undue influence was not, in fact, used. These relationships are:

(a)   religious advisor and advisee (as above);
(b)   doctor and patient;
(c)   solicitor and client;
(d)   teacher and pupil;
(e)   parent and child;
(f)   guardian and ward;
(g)   trustee and beneficiary.

Notes: (i) The relationship of husband and wife is not included. (ii) It is an equitable principle, i.e., a concept that originated in that branch of law developed in the former Court of Chancery and known as 'Equity'. Since 'delay defeats equity' (known as the doctrine of laches) the court — as in this case — may refuse to grant relief.

APPLESON v LITTLEWOOD LTD
[1939] 1 All ER 464

THE FACTS   The plaintiff sent in what he claimed was a winning football pools coupon entitling him to a prize of £4,335.

The defendant refused to pay, relying on a condition on the coupon which stated that: 'it shall not be attended by or give rise to any legal relationship, rights, duties, consequences . . .'.

THE DECISION   The plaintiff's claim failed. The condition indicated that the defendants had no intention to create legal relations.

COMMENTARY   There is a presumption that agreements of a domestic or social nature are not intended to be legally binding, whilst those of a business or commercial nature are intended to be legally binding.

These are not rules, merely presumptions, and presumptions can be rebutted, as in this case.

The arrangement between the parties appeared to be commercial in nature but the condition on the coupon operated to rebut the normal presumption and the transaction was not binding in law.

BAKER v HOPKINS LTD

[1959] 3 All ER 225

THE FACTS Hopkins Ltd were employed to clean out a well. It was decided to use a petrol-engined pump in the well and the two employees of Hopkins Ltd were instructed not to go down the well until all the engine fumes had cleared. However, both employees ignored this instruction, went down the well without waiting for the fumes to clear and were overcome by the fumes. Dr Baker was called to the well and he realised that if the lives of the two men were to be saved he could not wait for the arrival of the fire brigade, who had also been called. So Dr Baker had himself lowered on a rope down the well, only to find that the two men were already dead. The rope got caught and Dr Baker could not be raised out of the well in time to prevent him being overcome by the fumes as well.

Mrs Baker claimed in negligence for the loss of her husband, and Hopkins Ltd put up the defence of *volenti non fit injuria*, that is, that Dr Baker had consented to the risk of the harm that caused his death.

THE DECISION At first instance and on appeal it was held that, as Dr Baker was acting in the role of a rescuer, the maxim *volenti non fit injuria* was not applicable. Thus Mrs Baker's claim succeeded.

COMMENTARY This case illustrates that a rescuer is treated as a special case in English law, which has followed the law of the United States in this respect. Consequently, a rescuer cannot be regarded as having voluntarily accepted a risk of harm unless it would be wholly unreasonable to do so. Clearly any doctor in Dr Baker's position would have known that only very prompt action could prevent death from carbon monoxide poisoning.

BALFOUR v BALFOUR
[1919] 2 KB 571

THE FACTS   The defendant, a Civil Servant on leave in England, was due to return with his wife, the plaintiff, to Sri Lanka (Ceylon) when she became ill.

Mrs Balfour had to remain in England and her husband promised her a household allowance of £30 per month.

Later, the couple separated and Mrs Balfour sued for the allowance

THE DECISION   The agreement was in the nature of a domestic agreement. It relied on bonds of trust and affection but was not binding in law. The plaintiff was not legally entitled to the £30 per month.

COMMENTARY   For an agreement to be a contract the parties must have entered into it with 'the intention to create legal relations'. If this intention is absent, then the agreement is not legally binding, i.e., there is no contract.

This case illustrates the attitude the law takes towards agreements of a social or domestic nature; there is a presumption that such agreements are not intended to be legally binding. However, there are instances where the presumption does not apply; that is to say, 'there are cases where agreements which appear to be of a domestic character are legally binding. In such cases the presumption is said to be 'rebutted' (see, for example, *Simpkins* v *Pays*, p. 186).

BEALE v TAYLOR
[1967] 3 All ER 253

THE FACTS A private motorist advertised his car as: 'Herald Convertible, White, 1961, Twin Carbs'. The rear of the car carried figures '1200' to indicate the engine capacity. Another private motorist answered the advertisement, went to the seller's home and subsequently bought the car. Later the buyer discovered that the vehicle consisted of two halves welded together — the back half was a 1200cc model whereas the front half was from an earlier model with an inferior engine.

THE DECISION There was a breach of section 13 of the Sales of Goods Act 1893 which provides that 'where there is a contract for the sale of goods by description, there is an implied condition that the goods will correspond with the description'.

COMMENTARY A sale may be 'by description' even if the buyer (as in this case) has seen the goods. Even though the car was unroadworthy, the buyer could not bring an action under section 14(2) of the 1893 Act — the implied condition of 'merchantable quality' — since that section only applies to sales made 'in the course of a business'.

Note: the Sale and Supply of Goods Act 1994 which came into effect on 3 January 1995 reforms the terminology of the Sale of Goods Act 1979 (formerly the Sale of Goods Act 1893). It replaces the expression 'merchantable quality' with 'satisfactory quality'. The change is intended to explain more clearly that the implied condition as to quality covers all aspects of the goods including both aesthetic aspects (e.g., appearance and finish) and functional aspects (e.g., safety and durability).

BEARD v LONDON GENERAL OMNIBUS CO.
[1900] 2 QB 530

THE FACTS   The driver of a bus left it at the terminus and the bus conductor then drove it in order to turn the bus around. During the turning process the bus struck and injured Beard, who claimed compensation from the London General Omnibus Co. as the employer of the bus conductor who was driving the vehicle at the time of the accident.

THE DECISION   It was held by the Court of Appeal that the employer, London General Omnibus Co., was not liable to Beard for the actions of the bus conductor because their employee was not acting in the course of his employment as a bus conductor at the time of the accident.

COMMENTARY   The vicarious liability of an employer for the wrongs done by his employees has always been limited to liability for wrongs done during the course of the employment (see *Storey* v *Ashton*, p. 192).

This case illustrates that the courts may take a rather narrow view of the meaning of the expression 'during the course of the employment'. It may be wondered why Beard should not just have claimed against the bus conductor rather than the employer, but generally the employer is in a much better position to pay any compensation that may be awarded. Now that third party insurance is required for all vehicle drivers, the injured party would proceed against the insurers as well.

BELL v LEVER BROS
[1932] AC 161

THE FACTS Bell was employed by Lever Bros as managing director of one of their subsidiary companies. The subsidiary company was subsequently involved in a merger and under a redundancy agreement Lever Bros contracted to pay Bell £30,000 as compensation. Later they discovered that Bell had engaged in secret trading, an activity for which he could have been dismissed without compensation. Lever Bros sought to recover the £30,000 on the ground that the redundancy agreement was void due to mistake.

THE DECISION Lever Bros were unsuccessful, because they had got what they had bargained for, i.e., the termination of Bell's contract of employment.

The fact that they could have released Bell from his contract on much cheaper terms indicated a mistake as to quality and such a mistake does not render the contract void.

COMMENTARY The general rule is *caveat emptor* (let the buyer beware). This means, for instance, that if a buyer of a painting misjudges the value of the work and pays too much, that is his fault. He made a mistake as to quality and this does not invalidate the contract.

Lever Bros paid more than was necessary to obtain a redundancy agreement releasing Bell from his contract of employment. They made a mistake as to quality, for they could have dismissed him summarily without any 'golden handshake'. The result is the same — the redundancy agreement is not invalidated and Bell can keep the money.

Note: the court decided there was no fraud involved in the redundancy agreement.

BARON BERNSTEIN OF LEIGH v SKYVIEWS & GENERAL LTD
[1977] 2 All ER 902

THE FACTS   Without seeking permission, an aircraft belonging to Skyviews & General Ltd flew over Lord Bernstein's estate and took photographs of the house and grounds.

These photographs were subsequently offered for sale to Lord Bernstein, who sued in trespass on the basis that as owner of the land he was also the owner of the airspace above that land.

THE DECISION   It was held that there was no trespass at common law as a landowner's rights to the airspace above his property did not extend to an unlimited height. The court declined to lay down a height to which ownership of the airspace extends, saying that it was limited to the height necessary for the ordinary use and enjoyment of the land and buildings. In the airspace above that height the landowner had no greater rights than anyone else.

It was also held that even if there was a common-law trespass, the provisions of the Civil Aviation Act 1949 prevented any action being taken in respect of that trespass. Section 40 of the 1949 Act provides:

> No action shall lie in respect of trespass or in respect of nuisance, by reason only of the flight of an aircraft over any property at a height above the ground, which having regard to the wind and weather, and all the circumstances of the case is reasonable . . .

COMMENTARY   The limited ownership of the airspace above land in no way prevents landowners taking an action in trespass against signs, cranes and trees, etc., that invade their airspace. However, the landowner cannot take a trespass action against, say, a satellite that passes over his garden.

This case is a good example of common sense applied to the law. As the judge remarked, there being no law against the taking of photographs, Skyviews & General Ltd could take all the photographs they wished from outside the boundaries of Lord Bernstein's estate.

BENTLEY ENGINEERING CO. LTD v MISTRY
[1978] ICR 47

THE FACTS Mr Mistry was employed by Bentley Engineering as a timekeeper and he had a dispute about clocking-in procedures with another employee, Mr Singh, which led to a fight between the two employees. The fight was seen by other employees and was reported. Both employees were interviewed by the assistant personnel officer separately and both were suspended for a day. Each claimed that the other was entirely responsible for the incident. On return to work Mr Mistry was informed that he was to be dismissed; he appealed, in accordance with the company procedure, to the chief personnel officer, who interviewed both employees separately and read the statements made by the other employees who saw the incident. The decision to dismiss Mr Mistry was confirmed, so he applied to an Industrial Tribunal for compensation for unfair dismissal.

At the Tribunal, Bentley Engineering claimed that the dismissal was fair, but the claim for unfair dismissal was upheld on the grounds that Mr Mistry had no opportunity either to hear or question the complainant at the employer's domestic inquiries.

Bentley Engineering appealed against the decision of the Industrial Tribunal that the dismissal was unfair.

THE DECISION The Employment Appeal Tribunal upheld the decision of the Tribunal that the dismissal was unfair. It was held that natural justice required that the accused employee should have been given the opportunity by the employer, in the domestic inquiries, to hear what Mr Singh alleged had happened and to cross question Mr Singh on the allegations.

COMMENTARY The test any employer must satisfy when challenged about the fairness of the dismissal of an employee is: did the employer act reasonably in making the decision to dismiss?

This case suggests that if an employer does not conduct his domestic inquiries in accordance with natural justice, that is, fairly, then that employer does not act reasonably. There is a further problem when allegations of employee misconduct involve possible

BENTLEY ENGINEERING CO. LTD v MISTRY
— *continued*

criminal liability. It seems that the employer need not refer the allegations to the police, but may deal with the matter in accordance with his disciplinary process.

BISSET v WILKINSON
[1927] AC 177

THE FACTS The owner of farmland in New Zealand told a prospective purchaser of the farm that, in his opinion, it would 'carry 2,000 sheep'. The land had not previously been used as a sheep farm.

After buying the farm the purchaser discovered that it would only support a fraction of that number, so he sued for misrepresentation.

THE DECISION This was an honest statement of opinion which did not amount to a misrepresentation. The purchaser's claim failed.

COMMENTARY Misrepresentation is an untrue statement of fact which induces the contract, i.e., persuades the other party to enter the contract.

This case illustrates that a statement of belief or opinion cannot generally be a misrepresentation (assuming no fraud is involved). If the vendor in this case had said, 'It is a well-known fact that the land will support 2,000 sheep', he would have been liable in misrepresentation.

Note: silence cannot generally amount to misrepresentation. Suppose, for instance, that the vendor knew that the land was not suitable for sheep farming but did not say anything — there would be no misrepresentation. This reflects the general maxim *caveat emptor* (let the buyer beware). The effect is that a purchaser must make enquiries designed to elicit the information he needs to know. He should 'force' the vendor to make positive statements, e.g., 'The land will support 2,000 sheep.'

BLISS v HALL
(1838) 4 Bing NC 183

THE FACTS The plaintiff took up residence next to a tallow factory which for three years had manufactured candles.

The plaintiff sued in nuisance, complaining of the 'divers noisome, noxious and offensive vapours, fumes, smells and stenches' emitted by the factory.

THE DECISION There was an actionable nuisance. The plaintiff had a right to 'wholesome air' and it was no defence that the plaintiff came to the nuisance.

COMMENTARY Private nuisance is an unlawful interference with another's use or enjoyment of land, or some right over, or in connection with, it. Typical examples include noise, smoke, heat, smell, vibration, etc. It generally involves an element of repetition, e.g., one smoky bonfire does not entitle a neighbour to sue.

Lord Wright commented: 'A balance has to be maintained between the right of the occupier to do what he likes with his own, and the right of a neighbour not to be interfered with.'

Note: what is a nuisance in one area may not be a nuisance in another, e.g., a fish and chip shop may be a nuisance in a residential area but not in a commercial district. This is summed up in the dictum from the case *Sturges* v *Bridgman*, 'What may be a nuisance in Belgrave Square would not necessarily be so in Bermondsey'.

Nuisance is a wrong to occupation; it follows that a tenant can sue and be sued.

BOLTON v STONE
[1951] 1 All ER 1078

THE FACTS   While standing in a public road adjacent to a cricket ground, Miss Stone was struck and injured by a cricket ball that had been hit out of the ground during a match. The cricket ground was enclosed by a fence which was effectively 17 feet high where it separated the ground from the public road.

It was established that a ball had only been hit out of the ground into the public road on six occasions in the previous 30 years and that these incidents had not caused any injury or damage.

Miss Stone claimed in negligence against the cricket club and at first instance the claim was dismissed. On appeal the Court of Appeal upheld the claim, so the cricket club appealed to the House of Lords.

THE DECISION   In the judgment of the House of Lords, the standard of care in the law of negligence is the standard of the ordinarily careful man. The 'ordinarily careful man' does not take precautions against every foreseeable risk, only against risks which are reasonably likely to happen. Therefore the claim in negligence was dismissed.

COMMENTARY   This case highlights the difficult point that mere foreseeability of harm does not always give rise to a duty of care in the law of negligence. To the test of 'is it foreseeable?' has to be added a further test, 'what is the risk of the event happening?'. One of the Law Lords, Lord Reid, considered that a cricket ball escape on average once every five years was on the 'border line' of acceptable risk.

BOURHILL v YOUNG
[1943] AC 92

THE FACTS The plaintiff was eight months pregnant. She was alighting from a tram when she heard a collision in which a motorcyclist was killed. She did not see the accident but heard the collision and saw some blood on the road. She suffered nervous shock and gave birth to a stillborn child. Mrs Bourhill sued the personal representatives of the motorcyclist for his negligence.

THE DECISION The action failed as the injury to the plaintiff was not a reasonably foreseeable consequence of the motorcyclist's negligent driving.

COMMENTARY To be successful in an action in negligence the plaintiff must prove that the defendant:

(a) owed him a duty of care;
(b) was in breach of that duty;
(c) caused the injury to the plaintiff as a result.

A duty of care is owed to one's neighbour. In the tort of negligence a neighbour is anyone whom it may reasonably be anticipated will be affected by the act complained of.

The act complained of in this case was the motorcyclist's negligent driving which resulted in the fatal crash. He did not owe the plaintiff a duty of care since what happened could not have been anticipated, i.e., that a lady who did not see the accident would suffer nervous shock and give birth to a stillborn child.

Note: it is possible to recover damages for nervous shock in negligence. The case of *McLoughlin v O'Brian* (p. 114–15) illustrates that the courts are now prepared to make awards of damages for nervous shock to people who were not even at the scene of the accident. The case of *McLoughlin* should be read in conjunction with the later case on nervous shock of *Alcock v Chief Constable of South Yorkshire* (p. 21–2).

RE BRAVADA'S ESTATE
[1968] 2 All ER 217

THE FACTS The testator signed his will in the presence of four witnesses. Two of the witnesses were to benefit under the terms of the will and the testator only wished them to be present so that they would be aware of the will and its contents.

In 1968 the law governing signatures by 'interested' witnesses (i.e., those who would benefit under the terms of the will they were witnessing) was contained in section 15 of the Wills Act 1837.

THE DECISION Section 15 provided that a gift to a witness, or the husband or wife of a witness, was void, therefore although the will itself was valid, the gifts to the 'interested' witnesses were void, i.e., they could not receive their inheritance.

COMMENTARY The case is noteworthy not only because of the unusual facts and unfortunate consequence of a strict application of the 'letter of the law', but also as an illustration of the way in which Parliament can respond quickly to an obvious injustice.

Recognising that the intention of the testator had been thwarted, Parliament later in 1968 passed an amending Wills Act specifically to deal with future 'Bravada' situations. It provides that if there are two or more 'disinterested' witnesses, gifts to additional witnesses will be valid. Unfortunately, since legislation is not generally retrospective, it could not undo the fact that the two witnesses in the Bravada case had been disinherited by the prevailing rule of law.

BYRNE v DEANE
[1937] 2 All ER 204

THE FACTS A golf club provided illegal gaming machines for the use of the members. Someone informed the police of that fact and the gaming machines had to be removed. The following notice was put up in the place where the gaming machines had stood:

> For many years upon this spot
> You heard the sound of a merry bell
> Those who were rash and those who were not
> Lost and made a spot of cash
> But he who gave the game away
> May he byrnne in hell and rue the day

Byrne, a member of the club, claimed in defamation (libel), saying the words implied that he had informed the police, that he was disloyal, devoid of sporting spirit and not fit to be a member of the club; all of which damaged his reputation with other people.

At first instance Byrne was awarded nominal damages and costs, so the golf club appealed.

THE DECISION The Court of Appeal held that allegations of reporting unlawful actions to the police, whether true or false, cannot damage the reputation of a person in the opinion of 'right-thinking members of society'. Consequently Byrne had no claim in defamation.

COMMENTARY This case illustrates the basic defamation test, namely: does the allegation damage the reputation of the victim in the opinion of 'right-thinking members of society' and no one else?

CAMPBELL v PADDINGTON BOROUGH COUNCIL
[1911] 1 KB 869

THE FACTS The plaintiff let rooms overlooking the route for the funeral procession of King Edward VII. The defendants erected a stand which obstructed the highway and the view from the plaintiff's window. The plaintiff sued in the tort of public nuisance.

THE DECISION The plaintiff was entitled to damages for the profits which, but for the defentants' act, she would probably have made by letting rooms.

COMMENTARY Public nuisance is a crime. It becomes a tort as well where one person is affected more than the public in general.

The defendants in this case had obstructed the highway, which constitutes the crime of public nuisance. The plaintiff had been particularly affected and so could sue for the tort of public nuisance.

The classic type of public nuisance is interference with the public right of way along the highway, for example, by obstructing it or by making the way unsafe by erecting dangerous structures on or near the highway.

A plaintiff wishing to sue for the tort of public nuisance always has to show that he has suffered some special damage over and above that which is suffered by the public as a result of the nuisance, e.g., personal injury (a protruding lamp overhanging the highway fell and injured a passer-by), damage to property (maintenance to highway undermining foundations), loss of business profits (queues to theatre blocking entrance to shop), or inconvenience (loss of sleep due to traffic noise).

CAPPS v MILLER
[1989] 2 All ER 333

THE FACTS On the evening of 2 March 1985 Robin Capps, then aged 16, was riding his moped home and had stopped in the correct position in the centre of the road preparatory to making a right turn when he was struck by a following car driven by Miller. As a result of the collision Capps was thrown into the air and sustained very serious head injuries. Whilst Capps had been wearing a crash helmet this had not been securely fastened, as required by the Motor Cycles (Protective Helmets) Regulations 1980. Consequently, the helmet had become detached from the wearer before Capps hit the road surface (the helmet went through the windscreen of the car), so that it provided no protection against head injuries. The car driver, Miller, was found to be 72% over the permitted alcohol limit and was convicted of driving with an excess of alcohol.

Capps brought a claim against Miller in respect of his injuries and it was admitted that the accident was the fault of Miller who counterclaimed that Capps had been contributorily negligent in not securing his crash helmet as required by law.

At first instance it was held that the failure to secure the crash helmet did not reduce the liability of the car driver to any significant extent and the judge declined to apply the provisions of the Law Reform (Contributory Negligence) Act 1945 so as to reduce the damages awarded against the car driver. Miller appealed to the Court of Appeal against the refusal of the first instance judge to apportion blame and liability for the injuries sustained by Capps.

THE DECISION The Court of Appeal followed the decision in *Froom* v *Butcher* (a case involving the liability of a car passenger for not wearing his seat belt) and the judgment of Lord Denning MR, in that case. It was held that the failure to fasten a crash helmet, as required by law, was contributory negligence. The degree of blameworthiness attributable to Capps was 10% and his award of damages would be reduced by that percentage on the application of the Law Reform (Contributory Negligence) Act 1945.

COMMENTARY It is important to note that a distinction is drawn, in law, between blame for an accident itself and blame for the injuries that may result as a consequence of that accident. In this case Miller was 100% to blame for the collision between his car and Capps' moped but held to be only 90% to blame for the injuries sustained by Capps. Also note that, in fact, both parties were committing criminal offences although not on a scale comparable with that in the case of *Pitts* v *Hunt* (see p. 135–6).

CARLILL v THE CARBOLIC SMOKE BALL CO.

[1893] 1 QB 256

THE FACTS Mrs Carlill read an advertisement for a patent medicine known as a carbolic smoke ball. The advertisement made claims that the product would cure a number of ailments, including influenza. A reward of £100 was offered to anyone who caught influenza after using the smoke ball as directed. A sum of £1,000 was said to have been deposited in a bank to show the makers' 'sincerity in the matter'.

Mrs Carlill bought the smoke ball, using it for eight weeks as directed, but she still caught influenza and so claimed the £100 reward. The makers refused to pay the reward to Mrs Carlill, who then sued on the promise of the reward. The makers raised several defences to the claim by Mrs Carlill, including:

(a)   The reward offer was an attempt to contract with the entire world, which was not possible in English law.

(b)   The reward offer was a mere 'puff', there being no intention to enter into a binding legal obligation (no intention to create legal relations).

(c)   Mrs Carlill had not communicated her acceptance of the reward offer.

THE DECISION Mrs Carlill was entitled to the £100 reward because:

(a)   It was possible to make offers to the entire world where there was a promise by one party for an act by the other party (a unilateral contract).

(b)   The deposit of the £1,000 showed an intention to pay claims.

(c)   In unilateral contracts communication of acceptance was not necessary.

COMMENTARY This leading case establishes that in certain situations an offer, as well as an 'invitation to treat', can be made to the entire world. Thus 'price promise' offers, where a retailer offers a partial refund if his goods can be bought cheaper anywhere else within a certain time, can be enforced at law. This is the modern application of the *Carlill* case.

CASSIDY v DAILY MIRROR NEWSPAPERS LTD
[1929] 2 KB 331

THE FACTS The plaintiff was the wife of a man who was pictured with another woman in the defendants' newspaper under the heading 'Today's Gossip'. Beneath the picture was a statement that their engagement had recently been announced.

The plaintiff brought an action for defamation, claiming that there was an innuendo that she had been living 'in sin' with the man in the photograph, i.e., readers of the newspaper who knew her would conclude that if he had just become engaged to the woman in the photograph, he could not be married to her.

THE DECISION The photograph and statement were held to be defamatory of the plaintiff, since they contained the innuendo that she was not married to her husband. The plaintiff was awarded damages.

COMMENTARY An innuendo is a statement that is innocent on the face of it but which has a hidden defamatory meaning, e.g., 'Dr Brown drinks' might simply mean that the doctor likes mineral water but many people would draw the conclusion that the doctor drinks too much alcohol.

In cases where innuendo is claimed, it is up to the plaintiff to establish the hidden defamatory meaning.

Sometimes unintentional defamation occurs. This happens where a newspaper publishes an article that is true of one person but is taken to refer to another and is defamatory of him.

In general, a plaintiff wishing to be successful in an action for defamation must prove:

(a)   that the statement was defamatory, i.e., that it lowered him in the estimation of other reasonably minded people;

(b)   that the statement referred to him (or was taken by inference to refer to him, as in the above case);

(c)   that the statement was published, i.e., communicated to a third person;

(d)   that damage was suffered (in most cases).

CENTRAL LONDON PROPERTY TRUST LTD
v HIGH TREES HOUSE LTD
[1947] KB 130

THE FACTS   In 1937 the plaintiffs let to the defendants a block of flats at an annual rent of £2,500. The defendants in turn let each individual flat.

Following the outbreak of war the defendants found that they could not let all the flats and so the plaintiffs agreed in writing to a reduction in the annual rent of £1,250. No express time limit was set for the operation of this reduction. From 1940 to 1945 the defendants paid the reduced rent.

In 1945 the flats were full again and the plaintiffs brought an action claiming they were entitled to the original rent from 1945 onwards *and* submitting that they were entitled to the arrears of rent for the years 1940–1945. The basis of the claim was that there was no consideration for the agreement to reduce the rent, i.e., that it was a 'gratuitous waiver', which was not binding.

THE DECISION   The plaintiffs were entitled to revert to the original rent from 1945 since the abnormal wartime conditions no longer applied.

However, Denning J was of the opinion that any submission that they were entitled to the arrears would be defeated by the doctrine of *equitable estoppel.*

COMMENTARY   The case demonstrates how the doctrine of equitable estoppel may be applied to prevent someone going back on a 'waiver' (a promise to accept less than was originally owed). There are three conditions to be met before the doctrine will apply:

(a)   The promisor must waive his legal rights (i.e., give up some legal entitlement).
(b)   The waiver must be gratuitous (i.e., made for nothing).
(c)   The other party must alter his position in reliance on the waiver.

If all three conditions are fulfilled the plaintiff is 'estopped', or prevented, from going back on his word even though it was a promise made for nothing.

CENTRAL LONDON PROPERTY TRUST LTD
v HIGH TREES HOUSE LTD — *continued*

Note: the doctrine of estoppel is equitable and is based on fairness, so it cannot be used by a defendant to escape liability where he virtually holds the plaintiff to ransom, e.g., 'take £X or you'll get nothing'.

CHAPLIN v LESLIE FREWIN (PUBLISHERS) LTD
[1966] Ch 71

THE FACTS The plaintiff, the estranged son of Charlie Chaplin, signed a contract with the defendants for the publication of his autobiography while he was still a minor. Later he tried to avoid the contract, claiming it was not binding on him.

THE DECISION The contract was valid and binding. It was a beneficial contract of service which would enable him to earn his living and support his family.

COMMENTARY There are two classes of contract which bind a minor:

(a)   Necessaries (see *Nash* v *Inman*, p. 120).

(b)   Beneficial contracts of service: these are contracts which, taken as a whole, benefit the minor. The fact that the contract contains a harsh term will not necessarily mean it is void: if the remaining terms are in the minor's best interest, e.g., by enhancing his future prospects, the contract is valid. Hence beneficial contracts of service often involve the minor in education, training, apprenticeship, etc. (see *Roberts* v *Gray*, p. 180).

Note: the plaintiff in the above case was 19 when he made the contract. He was a minor because the age of majority was at that time 21. It was not until 1969 when the Family Law Reform Act was passed that the age of majority was reduced to 18. Prior to that piece of legislation anyone under the age of 21 was referred to, for contractual purposes, as an infant!

CHEESE v LOVEJOY

(1877) 37 LT 295

THE FACTS The testator drew a line through his will, wrote 'This is revoked' on it and kicked it into a pile of other papers in the corner of his room. His housekeeper picked it up and kept it in the kitchen for eight years until the testator's death. The next of kin claimed that it had been revoked.

THE DECISION The will could be admitted to probate. Section 20 of the Wills Act 1837 provides that a will may be revoked 'by burning, tearing or otherwise destroying the same by the testator, or by some person in his presence and by his direction, with the intention of revoking same'. Since the will had not been destroyed within the terms of section 20, it had not been revoked.

COMMENTARY For a will to be revoked by destruction, two conditions must be met:

(a) There must be a burning or tearing, i.e., cancellation by crossing out is insufficient.

(b) There must be an intention to revoke (an *animus revocandi*), i.e., destruction without an intention to revoke is insufficient. Thus a will which had been deposited in a solicitor's safe and was completely destroyed by fire during the blitz was admitted to probate supported by an affidavit as to its correctness (*Estate of Linfott*).

Note: a will may also be revoked by:

(a) a later will or codicil (provided it contains a 'revocation clause'):

(b) subsequent marriage.

CHRISTIE v DAVEY
[1893] 1 Ch 316

THE FACTS The parties lived in adjoining semi-detached houses. The defendant, exasperated by the music lessons and musical parties given by the plaintiff, retaliated by knocking on the wall, banging metal trays, whistling and shrieking!

The plaintiff sued in the tort of nuisance.

THE DECISION The defendant had acted maliciously and was liable. The plaintiff was granted an injunction.

COMMENTARY This case illustrates that motive may be relevant in nuisance. The courts, in judging what constitutes a nuisance, take into consideration the purpose of the defendant's activity. Acts which might otherwise be justified, may be regarded as unreasonable and a nuisance if done out of an improper motive such as malice or spite.

North J, in the above case, observed, 'if what has taken place had occurred between two sets of persons both perfectly innocent, I should have taken an entirely different view of the case'.

Consequently the mental state of the defendant may make his conduct nuisance, although had that mental state been different, nuisance would not have been committed. For example, a defendant who encouraged his son to discharge guns on his land with the intention that the noise would interfere with the breeding of the plaintiff's silver foxes was held liable in nuisance.

Note: the law recognises that a certain amount of discomfort is inevitable in life owing to the activities of one's neighbours but also expects that neighbours will lessen this discomfort as much as they are able, i.e., there must be a certain amount of 'give and take'.

CHRISTIE v DAVEY

'retaliated by knocking on the wall, banging metal trays ...'

COLLINS v GODEFROY
(1831) 1 B & Ad 950

THE FACTS   The plaintiff had received a subpoena requiring him to attend court as a witness for the defendant. The defendant promised to pay him six guineas. The defendant subsequently refused to pay and the plaintiff sued.

THE DECISION   The plaintiff was unsuccessful. In attending court, he was only doing what he was already legally obliged by the subpoena to do. Consequently he was not providing any consideration in exchange for the defendant's promise to pay — so the agreement was not binding.

COMMENTARY   Consideration is a necessary element in the formation of a valid simple contract. The classic definition of consideration was expressed in the case of *Currie* v *Misa* as 'some right, interest, profit or benefit accruing to one party, or some forbearance, detriment, loss or responsibility given, suffered or undertaken by the other'. In other words, it is the exchange value in the contract — both parties must 'give up' or sacrifice something in exchange for what they receive.

It follows that a promise to perform an existing duty is not consideration since nothing has been 'sacrificed'. Collins had not sacrificed anything as he had to attend court — regardless of the six guineas. If he had not received the subpoena then his time and trouble in attending court would have been his consideration.

Vague promises, e.g., 'to do the right thing', do not constitute consideration, likewise agreements made 'in consideration of natural love and affection'.

CONDOR v THE BARRON KNIGHTS LTD
[1966] 1 WLR 87

THE FACTS The plaintiff was a drummer in the Barron Knights band. He had a five-year contract which required him to play on seven nights a week when the band had engagements. He fell ill and was advised by his doctor that he was only fit to play on four nights a week. Consequently the band terminated his contract of employment.

THE DECISION The contract was frustrated (brought to an end/discharged). In the business sense it was impossible for the plaintiff to continue his contract so it was properly terminated.

COMMENTARY A contract is frustrated when the contract has become impossible to perform. When this happens the party who has been prejudiced is released from his legal obligation to fulfil the contract.

This case illustrates that one of the events that may frustrate a contract is personal injury in a contract for personal services.

Contracts discharged on this ground have included: an agreement to perform at a concert; an agreement to serve an apprenticeship of a fixed duration.

Note: (i) Frustration of contract may be referred to as supervening or subsequent impossibility. (ii) A contract is not frustrated merely because it has become more difficult to fulfil the contract (see *Davis Contractors Ltd v Fareham Urban District Council,* p. 59).

COOK v SQUARE D LTD
The Times, 23 October 1991

THE FACTS Mr Cook was an electronics service engineer who frequently worked abroad. In 1982 Mr Cook was working for Square D Ltd on a 4 computer control system in Saudi Arabia owned by Aramco. Just before completing his work, Mr Cook injured his leg when he slipped into a small opening in the floor of the computer control room which had been left unguarded.

Mr Cook claimed damages in respect of his injury from his employer, Square D Ltd, on the basis that the employer had failed in its duty of care to ensure that a safe system of work was provided for its employee.

At first instance Mr Cook was awarded damages against his employer, Square D Ltd. Square D Ltd appealed to the Court of Appeal.

THE DECISION It would not be reasonable to hold the employers in breach of their duty of care to their employee because of a hazard created by others some 8,000 miles away. Accordingly, the award of damages to Mr Cook would be set aside.

As Farquharson LJ put it:

The suggestion that the home based employers had any responsibility for the daily events of a site in Saudi Arabia had an air of unreality.

COMMENTARY In general an employer cannot evade his responsibility for the safety of his employees by saying that he delegated this to another whom he reasonably thought was competent. This case illustrates that there are limits to an employer's obligations and it might well be a very different matter if a UK employer sent a number of his employees to work abroad, for in those circumstances the employer might be under an obligation to satisfy himself that the site his employees would be working at was safe.

The state of the employment protection laws is not entirely satisfactory with regard to UK employees working abroad.

COPE v SHARPE
[1912] 1 KB 496

THE FACTS A fire broke out on the plaintiff's land. The defendant, a gamekeeper, entered his land and lit some heather to create a 'fire break' to protect nesting pheasants belonging to his employer. The plaintiff sued in trespass.

THE DECISION The defence of necessity applied and the gamekeeper was not liable. There was a real and imminent danger to the game and what he did was reasonably necessary.

COMMENTARY Necessity is one of the general defences to an action in tort. It applies where the defendant reasonably responds to a danger by taking action intended to prevent a greater peril, e.g., destroying a building damaged by fire to prevent its collapse on to the highway.

The necessity must be judged at the time of the defendant's action. In the above case the gamekeeper's action was justified by the circumstances at the time even though the fire actually died out before reaching his employer's land.

Necessity may, in certain circumstances, be a justification for inflicting harm on a person. In *Leigh* v *Gladstone* it was decided that person warders who forcibly fed the plaintiff, a suffragette on hunger strike in prison, were not liable for the tort of battery.

Similarly, a surgeon who performs a life-saving operation without obtaining consent may claim this defence.

CORBETT v CORBETT
[1970] 2 All ER 654

THE FACTS   A man had a sex change operation and changed his name to April Ashley. April Ashley 'married' a man and the couple lived together. Then the husband asked for the marriage to be declared void.

THE DECISION   The marriage was not valid because the sex change operation had not altered Ashley's legal sex with which he had been born.

COMMENTARY   Section 11(c) of the Matrimonial Causes Act 1973 (reflecting Lord Penzance's definition of marriage in *Hyde* v *Hyde* (p. 92) requires the parties to a marriage to be respectively male and female. The judge in *Corbett* v *Corbett* (who was also a qualified medical practitioner) declared the marriage void since the petitioner was a man and so, at birth, was the respondent. Thus, as far as English law is concerned, it is not the psychological gender that determines a person's sex but the biological sex and this is fixed at birth and cannot be changed by artificial means.

COTTON v DERBYSHIRE DALES DISTRICT COUNCIL
The Times, 20 June 1994

THE FACTS   On Easter Monday 1984 Mr Cotton and some friends were out walking on High Tor, Matlock. The group started to walk down very steep and dangerous ground leading to a sheer drop. Mr Cotton fell over the cliff and sustained serious injuries.

Mr Cotton claimed damages from the District Council on the basis that, as owners and occupiers of the land, the Council had breached the duty of care for the safety of visitors to their land imposed on them by the Occupiers Liability Act 1957, by failing to provide warning notices of the dangerous cliff.

At first instance the claim was dismissed, so Mr Cotton appealed to the Court of Appeal.

THE DECISION   The Court of Appeal upheld the first instance dismissal of the claim. It was held that an occupier of land was under no duty to provide warning notices of *obvious* dangers so there was no breach of the requirements of the Occupiers Liability Act 1957. Their Lordships ruled that any visitor to High Tor exercising reasonable care for their own safety when walking down very steep and dangerous ground could have turned back before reaching the cliff *even through the cliff might not have been visible at the start of the descent.*

COMMENTARY   Students may feel this case poses the problem, when is a danger obvious?. Clearly it is not necessary to warn against the dangers of, say, sitting down on a motorway, but there is a 'grey' area between dangers which are obvious and dangers which are not.

COUTURIER v HASTIE
(1853) 156 ER 43

THE FACTS Hastie, merchants in Smyrna, sent a cargo of corn by sea from Salonica to England. Couturier, in London, was employed as an agent to resell the corn on the basis that he would make good any loss due to default in the resale contract (a *del credere* agent).

Couturier sold on the corn, while it was in transit, to Callender. It was then discovered that the corn had been sold en route by the captain of the ship when the corn became overheated. Callender then repudiated the contract of sale on the basis that at the time of sale to him the corn no longer existed. Thus Couturier could become liable to Hastie for the purchase price promised by Callender.

THE DECISION At first instance it was held that the contract of resale of the corn was valid. On appeal to the Court of Appeal (subsequently affirmed by the House of Lords) it was held that there was no valid contract of resale as at the time of contracting, unknown to the parties, the corn had ceased to exist as such.

COMMENTARY Note that this case had its title reversed in the course of progress through the courts, starting as *Hastie* v *Couturier*.

In this rather confusing case it should be borne in mind that Couturier, as the reselling agent, could be liable for the default of the purchaser if the contract he arranged with the purchaser, Callender, was held valid. This old case is often cited as authority for the proposition that a mistake about the existence of the subject-matter of a contract results in there being no contract, as the parties are not in true agreement.

CUNDY v LINDSAY
(1878) 3 App Cas 459

THE FACTS   A rogue named Blenkarn ordered goods by post from the defendants, signing the order 'Blenkiron & Co.', a genuine company known to the defendants.

Blenkarn received the goods and sold them to Cundy.

Lindsay & Co. successfully sued Cundy for the return of the goods. Cundy appealed.

THE DECISION   There had been an operative mistake as to the identity of the other party (Blenkarn). Such a mistake renders the contract void. Since the contract between Blenkarn and Lindsay & Co. was void, Cundy could not obtain legal title, i.e., ownership of the goods, for title cannot pass under a void contract.

COMMENTARY   Mistakes take many forms.

Certain mistakes render the contract void. These are known as 'operative' mistakes. A mistake that does not affect the validity of a contract is known as an 'inoperative' mistake.

A mistake as to the identity of the other party to a contract may be operative or inoperative.

The general rule is that where the parties are dealing on a 'face to face' basis, the contract will not be void for mistake, merely voidable for misrepresentation.

This case demonstrates that where the parties are not dealing on a face to face basis, e.g., through the post, the original contract (Blenkarn/Lindsay & Co.) *is* void for mistake, so any subsequent contract (Blenkarn/Cundy) cannot pass title to the goods, i.e., ownership remains with the party who was the victim of mistaken identity (Lindsay & Co.).

CUTLER v UNITED DAIRIES LTD
[1933] 2 KB 297

THE FACTS   The plaintiff was injured whilst trying to pacify a milkman's horse which had bolted into a field. He sued for negligence.

The defendants sought to rely on the defence *volenti non fit injuria* ('no injury can be done to a willing person' or 'he who consents cannot complain').

THE DECISION   The defence was successful.

The plaintiff's action failed, as he had voluntarily undertaken the risk and the hazards that went with it.

COMMENTARY   The defence in the law of tort known as *volenti* can be used against a volunteer or rescuer who is injured whilst attempting a rescue.

The defence will not be successful where the rescuer was acting under a moral or legal duty to preserve life, e.g., a doctor (see *Baker* v *Hopkins Ltd*, p. 25) or a policeman (*Haynes* v *Harwood*).

In the *Cutler* case, the plaintiff was merely a by-stander alerted by the milkman's cries for help in a situation which presented no danger to others. In the *Haynes* case, the plaintiff was a policeman who was attempting to stop a runaway horse in a crowded street.

DAVIS CONTRACTORS LTD v FAREHAM URBAN DISTRICT COUNCIL
[1956] 2 All ER 145

THE FACTS In 1946 Davis offered to build 78 houses for Fareham Council in eight months for £92,425 subject to adequate labour and material supplies being available. The subsequent formal contract between the parties contained no mention of the offer term regarding the availability of labour and material. Due to labour and material shortages the houses took 22 months to complete and the cost increased by £17,651.

Davis claimed that their offer term about availability of labour and material was incorporated in the formal contract although not expressly stated in writing; also that the contract was frustrated by the delay, consequently they could recover the additional cost (£17,651) as an extra to the contract price (£92,425) which was no longer binding on them.

THE DECISION At first instance it was held that the offer term was a term of the formal contract and that Davis could recover the additional cost. On appeal to the Court of Appeal (subsequently affirmed by the House of Lords) it was held that the offer term was not incorporated in the formal contract, that the extra cost could not be recovered and that the contract was not frustrated by the delay.

COMMENTARY The House of Lords when considering what events frustrate a contract made it clear that difficulties resulting from the delayed performance of a contract do not frustrate the contract if those difficulties could have been readily anticipated and provided for, as in this case.

DE FRANCESCO v BARNUM
(1890) 45 Ch D 430

THE FACTS The defendant, a 14-year-old girl, entered into a contract with the plaintiff to be taught stage dancing. The contract stipulated that she would not marry during the contract and that she would not accept professional engagements without the plaintiff's permission.

THE DECISION The contract was void.

It was not a beneficial contract of service. Whilst it was in the nature of an apprenticeship, the terms were so harsh (onerous) that 'the child was at the absolute disposal of the plaintiff'. It could not therefore be regarded as beneficial.

COMMENTARY Where a minor enters into a 'beneficial contract of service' it is binding on him, i.e., it is a valid contract which can be enforced by him and against him. Contracts for education, training or apprenticeship generally fall within this category.

This case demonstrates, however, that such contracts must be looked at as a whole. If the contract is predominantly in the minor's best interest then, despite an isolated onerous term, it is binding on him. If, on the other hand, it is predominantly harsh then, despite a beneficial aspect (such as being taught stage dancing), it is not binding.

DERRY v PEEK

[1886–90] All ER Rep 1

THE FACTS The Plymouth, Devonport & District Tramway Co. operated horse-drawn trams under a private Act of Parliament. The Act provided that, subject to the approval of the Board of Trade, steam or mechanical trams could be used.

The directors of the Tramway Company offered shares for sale, their prospectus stating: 'One great feature of this undertaking, to which considerable importance should be attached, is that, by special Act of Parliament obtained, the company has the right to use steam or mechanical motive power, instead of horses, and it is fully expected that by this means a considerable saving will result . . .'. Sir Henry Peek, acting in reliance on this statement, bought shares in the Tramway Company.

Later the Board of Trade refused consent to the use of steam or mechanical power, the Company was wound up and the shareholders lost money. Sir Henry sued the directors for fraudulent misrepresentation, claiming that the statement in their prospectus had induced him to buy shares in the Company. At first instance the claim was rejected but on appeal the Court of Appeal upheld the claim, so the directors further appealed to the House of Lords.

THE DECISION It was held that a misrepresentation was only fraudulent if:

(a) it was made knowing that it was untrue; *or*
(b) it was made without belief in its truth; *or*
(c) it was made recklessly, that is, not caring if it was true or false.

Whilst the prospectus was inaccurate, the directors honestly thought that the Board of Trade consent was a formality, so their misrepresentation was not fraudulent. The House of Lords reversed the decision of the Court of Appeal — the directors were not liable to Sir Henry Peek.

COMMENTARY This is one of the leading cases on fraudulent misrepresentation but the circumstances are not likely to recur, since directors who issue a prospectus now have a statutory duty for its accuracy under the Companies Acts.

DICKINSON v DODDS
(1876) 2 Ch D 463

THE FACTS On 10 June 1874 Dodds delivered by hand to Dickinson a written offer to sell certain properties. The offer stated: 'This offer to be left over until Friday, 9 o'clock a.m. June 12 1874.' During the afternoon of 11 June Dickinson was informed by an estate agent that Dodds was in negotiations with another person for the sale of the properties.

At 7.00 p.m. on 11 June Dickinson delivered to the residence of Dodds, by hand, a letter of acceptance for the properties, which it seems was never seen by Dodds. At 7.00 a.m. on 12 June the estate agent, acting for Dickinson, delivered to Dodds personally a duplicate written acceptance by Dickinson for the properties. It then transpired that Dodds had contracted with the other person for the sale of the properties on the afternoon of 11 June.

At first instance Dickinson was awarded a decree of specific performance against Dodds (an order to Dodds to sell the properties to Dickinson). Dodds appealed.

THE DECISION The Court of Appeal held that the order of specific performance should be set aside, as it must have been perfectly obvious to Dickinson before he accepted the offer from Dodds that Dodds had changed his mind and might be contemplating offering his properties to another. Thus Dickinson had notice, through a third party (the estate agent) that the offer by Dodds was revoked. The fact that Dickinson did not receive notice of revocation directly from Dodds was not material.

COMMENTARY This case answers a question about which there is often misunderstanding, namely that in the law of contract a promise which is made gratis (i.e., for nothing) cannot be enforced unless made under seal.

Dickinson did not buy the promise by Dodds to keep the offer open until a certain time; it would have been very different if Dickinson had paid Dodds for his promise, for then Dickinson would have had a binding option to purchase the properties.

It is unwise to rely on any promise given gratis, especially one involving the sale of property.

DIRECTOR OF PUBLIC PROSECUTIONS v NEWBURY AND JONES

[1976] 2 All ER 365

THE FACTS   The guard of a local train from Pontyp-ridd to Cardiff was sitting next to the driver. As the train approached a bridge over the line Newbury and Jones (both aged about 15) pushed a large piece of concrete off the parapet of the bridge. The piece of concrete hit the front of the driver's compartment of the train, killing the guard.

Newbury and Jones were convicted of manslaughter and the conviction was upheld on appeal by the Court of Appeal. Newbury and Jones further appealed to the House of Lords on the grounds that a person could not be convicted of manslaughter if he did not foresee the harm his action might cause; that is, he did not foresee that the action was dangerous.

THE DECISION   The House of Lords held that persons who carry out unlawful and dangerous acts which harm others are liable for manslaughter if their action results in death.

Foresight of the risk of harm to others is not material. How dangerous the action in question may be is to be decided by the objective test — would the 'man in the street' have recognised the action as dangerous — not did the wrongdoer recognise that action as dangerous. The conviction was upheld.

COMMENTARY   This case illustrates the 'unlawful and dangerous act' type of manslaughter.

Note that there are two elements in such cases, namely: an unlawful act which is also a dangerous act *in the view of the man in the street* and not in the view of the wrongdoer. The unlawful act in this case was, of course, attempting to obstruct the rail track contrary to British Rail by-laws.

DOBSON v GENERAL ACCIDENT
ASSURANCE plc
[1989] 3 All ER 927

THE FACTS Mr Dobson insured the contents of his house, including items of high value, with General Accident against the usual risks including 'loss by theft'. In November 1987 Mr Dobson advertised a gold watch and a diamond ring for sale for £5,950. An unknown person telephoned Mr Dobson and expressed interest in buying the items at the asking price, it being agreed that payment would be by means of a building society cheque. The next day the unknown person called on Mr Dobson and collected the watch and ring in exchange for a cheque for £5,950 from the Birmingham Midshires Building Society in favour of Mr Dobson. The cheque was returned unpaid as it had been stolen. Mr Dobson made a claim under his insurance for the loss by theft of the watch and ring. General Accident rejected the claim so Mr Dobson took proceedings against his insurers.

At first instance it was held that there had been a theft of the insured items and that General Accident were liable. The insurers appealed to the Court of Appeal on the grounds that:

(a) The property in the watch and ring passed to the stranger at the time of the telephone agreement for their sale so at the time of appropriation on the next day the items were 'not the property of another' (Mr Dobson) as required by the Theft Act 1968.

(b) As Mr Dobson had allowed the stranger to take the items there had been no adverse interference with or usurpation of the owner's rights, held by the House of Lords in R v Morris to be necessary to establish an 'appropriation'.

THE DECISION It was held that in the circumstances the property in the watch and ring was intended to pass to the stranger only upon receipt of a buiding society cheque, therefore the property in the articles passed at the time of delivery which was also the time of appropriation. Consequently, the articles were the 'property of another' at the time of appropriation. It was also held that an 'appropriation' could occur even if the owner

DOBSON v GENERAL ACCIDENT ASSURANCE plc — *continued*

consented to the property being taken and it followed that there was an adverse interference with or usurpation of the rights of the owner.

The stranger had dishonestly appropriated property belonging to another and had committed theft. Accordingly, General Accident were liable for the loss of the insured items.

COMMENTARY For the case of *R* v *Morris* refer to p. 164. Previous decisions on theft of property obtained by strangers using dud cheques have involved consideration of whether the contract of sale with the stranger was void (never existed) or voidable (existed until set aside). Property cannot pass under a void contract but does pass under a voidable contract until that contract is set aside. The judicial approach now seems to be to regard the status of the contract as irrelevant.

'a glass of ginger beer'

DONOGHUE (OR M'ALISTER) v STEVENSON
[1932] AC 562

THE FACTS   A lady was given a glass of ginger beer to drink, which had been poured out of an opaque glass type of bottle, thus preventing the contents from being seen. Later, when the rest of the ginger beer was poured from the bottle, the contents were seen to be contaminated with the decomposing remains of a dead snail.

The realisation by the lady that she had consumed contaminated ginger beer caused her nervous shock and subsequent gastric illness. A claim for compensation for the negligence of the manufacturer of the ginger beer was rejected at first instance and on appeal, so there was a further appeal to the House of Lords.

THE DECISION   By a majority the House of Lords held that:

> Every person has a legal duty of care to avoid acts or omissions which can reasonably be foreseen as likely to injure a 'neighbour'.

It was also held that, in law, a 'neighbour' is any person who could be so affected by the act (or omission) that they ought reasonably to be in the mind of the doer of that act (or omission) when it is thought about. The claim for compensation was upheld.

COMMENTARY   This is the leading case on negligence and has already become one of the most important judicial decisions of the century. From this very ordinary situation the principle was established that all persons may owe a legal duty of care not to do anything that can be foreseen as likely to harm others.

It is essential to note that the extent of the duty of care is limited by the test of *foreseeability of harm*; where the harm could not have been foreseen it is said to be 'too remote'.

In this case also note that the injured party was *given* the ginger beer, so there was no contractual relationship with either the seller or the manufacturer of the contaminated ginger beer, consequently no claim in contract was possible.

67

DONOGHUE (OR M'ALISTER) v STEVENSON
— *continued*

Many providers of services now attempt to limit liability for their negligence, sometimes by international agreement, as in the case of the airlines. Such limitations are subject to statutory controls.

DORI v RECREB SRL
C-91/92, 14 July 1994, ECJ

THE FACTS Commission Directive 85/577 to Italy and other Member States required that domestic consumer protection laws should include, by 1987, a right for consumers who entered into contracts away from business premises to have not less than seven days in which to cancel such contracts. Consumer law in Italy was not changed to comply with the Directive until 1992.

In January 1989 Ms Dori signed a contract with an associated company of Recreb, at Milan railway station, for an English language correspondence course. Four days later Ms Dori gave notice by registered post that she wished to cancel the contract. Recreb applied to the Giudice Conciliatore court for an order that Ms Dori pay the agreed sum plus costs, which was granted. Ms Dori objected on the basis that the Directive, although not implemented by Italy at the material time, conferred upon her the seven-day period in which to cancel the contract. The court stayed the proceedings and referred to the European Court of Justice for a ruling.

THE DECISION Under Article 189 of the Treaty of Rome a Directive was only binding on the Member States to which it was addressed. Consequently, a Directive could not, of itself, impose obligations on an individual and could not therefore be relied upon against an individual. If the Directive had not been transposed into national law within the prescribed time limit, consumers could not enforce the provisions of the Directive. However, the national court, when applying existing domestic law, should have regard to the purpose of the Directive.

COMMENTARY This case confirms that a Directive does not confer a right of action by one individual against another individual (known as the 'horizontal' effect). In such circumstances a Directive is said to be *not directly applicable*.

Compare this case with *Francovich* v *Italian State* [1992] (p. 77) where a Directive was held to confer rights of action by an individual against his State (known as 'vertical' effect).

69

DUDLEY METROPOLITAN BOROUGH COUNCIL
v DEBENHAMS PLC
The Times, 16 August 1994

THE FACTS A trading standards officer from Dudley Council entered a Debenham store to make a routine inspection, inter alia, for possible breaches of section 20 of the Consumer Protection Act 1987, which provides:

> ... a person shall be guilty of an offence if, in the course of any business of his, he gives (by any means whatever) to any consumers an indication which is misleading as to the price at which any goods, services, accommodation or facilities are available ...

A record of the store sales was requested and, subsequently Debenhams were charged with eight offences under section 20 of the 1987 Act.

The Justices declined to hear the charges on the basis that the trading standards officer had not complied with the requirements of Code B of the Codes of Practice issued under section 66 of the Police and Criminal Evidence Act 1984.

Code B provides that when searches are made by consent the person concerned must be given written notice that there is no obligation to consent to a search. Dudley Council appealed to the Divisional Court of Queen's Bench by way of case stated.

THE DECISION The Divisional Court held that whilst the trading standards officer had entered the store lawfully, the power under section 29 of the Consumer Protection Act to require the production of business records could not have been invoked as there were no grounds to suspect that any offence(s) had been committed. Consequently, records could only be obtained with consent.

The court further held that the fact of entry and 'looking about' constituted a 'search' and it was not necessary for there to be any physical interference with goods. Hence, the provisions of Code B of the Codes of Practice were applicable and a failure to observe the Code entitled the Justices to decline to hear the charges.

The appeal was dismissed.

DUDLEY METROPOLITAN BOROUGH COUNCIL v DEBENHAMS PLC — *continued*

COMMENTARY This case provides an interpretation of the meaning of 'search' which does not quite accord with the usual meaning given to the word.

It seems that trading standards officers will have to carry copies of the required notice regarding consent to 'searches' to present to shopkeepers, unless there are reasonable grounds for suspecting an offence has been committed when the statutory powers are available.

ESSO PETROLEUM v HARPER'S GARAGES LTD
[1967] 1 All ER 699

THE FACTS Harper's owned two garages, each of which sold petrol and oils, etc. In 1962 and 1963 Harper's entered into agreements with Esso that only Esso petrol and oils would be purchased for sale at both garages ('solus' agreements). One agreement was to run for 4½ years and the other agreement was to run for 21 years. During 1964 Harper's began to sell other brands of petrol and oils at both garages, so Esso sought an injunction to prevent Harper's from breaking their 'solus' agreements.

Injunctions were granted at first instance but set aside on appeal by the Court of Appeal on the grounds that the 'solus' agreements were in restraint of trade and illegal. Esso further appealed to the House of Lords.

THE DECISION The House of Lords held that agreements that restrain trade are only enforceable if the restraint could be justified.

The purpose of the 'solus' agreements so far as Esso were concerned was to ensure a stable system of distribution for their products, and this was a legitimate interest that Esso were entitled to protect for a reasonable length of time.

In the opinion of all of the members of the House of Lords 4½ years was a reasonable length of time for a 'solus' agreement to operate but 21 years was an unreasonable length of time for such an agreement to run. The injunction was restored in respect of the 4½-year agreement, and the setting aside of the injunction was confirmed in respect of the 21-year agreement.

COMMENTARY This leading case indicates that some restraint of trade provisions in agreements are lawful and do not render such agreements void. In the case of garages it should be borne in mind that petrol suppliers often provide financial assistance to the garage owner in return for a 'solus' agreement covering the supply of petrol and oils, etc.

FELTHOUSE v BINDLEY
(1862) 142 ER 1037

THE FACTS The plaintiff wrote offering to buy his nephew's horse for £30 and added: 'If I hear no more about him, I consider the horse mine at that price.' The nephew did not reply but did instruct the defendant, an auctioneer, to withdraw the horse from a forthcoming sale of his stock. The defendant did not do so and the horse was sold at auction to a third party.

The plaintiff sued the auctioneer in the tort of conversion.

THE DECISION The plaintiff had not contracted to buy the horse, as 'silence cannot amount to acceptance'. It followed that the horse did not belong to the plaintiff, so he could not sue the auctioneer for conversion.

COMMENTARY This is an instance where a principle in the law of contract determined the outcome of a case in another branch of law, namely the tort of conversion. Conversion is an unjustifiable interference with another's ownership of goods.

The plaintiff would only succeed if he demonstrated that his ownership had been interfered with. He failed as he did not have ownership. This was established by the application of the contractual principle that 'silence cannot amount to acceptance', i.e., he could not claim that his offer of £30 for the horse had been accepted, for his nephew's silence could not, in law, be regarded as acceptance.

This case may be distinguished from *Carlill* v *The Carbolic Smoke Ball Co. Ltd* (p. 42). In the *Carlill* case the *defendants* dispensed with the need to communicate acceptance, i.e., an offeror may dispense with the need to communicate acceptance but he may not — as in *Felthouse* v *Bindley* — arbitrarily impose contractual liability upon an offeree merely by proclaiming that silence shall be deemed consent.

FISHER v BELL
[1961] 1 QB 394

THE FACTS The defendant displayed a flick-knife with a price tag attached in his shop window. It was a criminal offence to 'offer for sale' certain offensive weapons, including flick-knives.

The defendant was prosecuted.

THE DECISION The defendant was acquitted. He had not 'offered for sale' the flick-knife, as its display was merely an invitation to treat. An invitation to treat is not an offer, simply an invitation to the other party to make an offer.

COMMENTARY This is an instance where a principle in the law of contract determined the outcome of a case in another branch of law, namely criminal law.

The court could not convict the defendant, as he did not come within the wording of the offence, i.e., he had not *offered* for sale the flick-knife since its display was, in law, an invitation to treat.

Other examples of an invitation to treat include:

— goods on 'self-service' shelves;
— newspaper advertisements;
— TV advertisements;
— an auctioneer asking for bids;
— transport timetables;
— wine lists.

FITCH v DEWES
[1921] 2 AC 158

THE FACTS A solicitor's managing clerk took employment with a Tamworth firm of solicitors for three years; the contract of employment contained the following term: 'The managing clerk shall not be engaged or manage or be concerned in the office, profession, or business of a solciitor within a radius of seven miles of the Town Hall of Tamworth.'

On leaving this employment the managing clerk sought to challenge the validity of the term as being in restraint of trade, since being without any time limit it amounted to a life-long prohibition on him working in Tamworth.

THE DECISION Although unlimited in time, the restriction would be enforced, as it did not exceed what was reasonably required to protect the 'trade secrets' (identity, etc., of clients) of the employing solicitors and the restriction was not contrary to the public interest.

COMMENTARY This decision is still relied upon; many firms of solicitors employ their staff on condition that they do not work for any other firm of soliitors within the seven-mile radius.

It is unusual for terms in restraint of trade to be unlimited in time but perhaps the legal profession is a special case, as so many clients of established firms of solicitors have placed their legal work with the same firm for very many years.

FOSTER v MACKINNON
(1869) LR 4 CP 704

THE FACTS The plaintiff was the holder of a bill of exchange for £3,000 which had been endorsed by the defendant.

The defendant had been induced to sign the bill by a third party named Callow, who told him that it was a guarantee.

The bill was later negotiated to the plaintiff who took it in ignorance of the fraud. He sued the defendant as endorser of the bill.

THE DECISION The plaintiff was unsuccessful. The defendant was not liable on the bill.

An old man of feeble sight, he had not been negligent in signing the bill. The document he signed was fundamentally different from the document he thought he was signing, so the defence of *non est factum* applied.

COMMENTARY *Non est factum* means 'it is not my act/deed'. This defence is based on the principle that a contract is not binding where the essential ingredient of consent is lacking.

The plea of *non est factum* is only available within narrow limits. The defendant must establish that:

(a) The document which he signed was fundamentally different as regards character or effect from the document he thought he was signing (a bill of exchange is different in character from a guarantee).

(b) He was not careless (Mackinnon, being senile and poor-sighted, was held not to have been negligent).

FRANCOVICH v ITALIAN STATE

ECJ [1992] C-9/90

THE FACTS The Euro Council issued a Directive (80/987) to Member States requiring provision of domestic law to ensure that when an employer became insolvent and unable to pay wages, these would be guaranteed by *guarantee institutions*.

Mr Francovich was employed by CDN Elettronica who became insolvent when owing Mr Francovich 6,000,000 lire (about £2,500) in wages. However, Italy had failed to implement Directive 80/987 so Mr Francovich claimed the 6,000,000 lire from the Italian Government. The case was referred to the Euro Court for a ruling.

THE DECISION The Euro Court held that the Italian Government could not be sued in debt as the Directive did not specify *who* would guarantee wage payments. However, the Italian State could be liable for failure to carry out the Directive if:

(a) the Directive conferred rights on individuals;
(b) the Directive clearly defined the rights conferred;
(c) a link existed between the damage suffered by the individual and the failure of the State to implement the Directive.

As all three conditions were fulfilled in this case, Mr Francovich was entitled to damages as a matter of Community law.

COMMENTARY The claim was effectively upheld as a liability in tort.

Compare this case with *Dori v Recreb Srl* [1994] (p. 69) where failure to implement a Directive did not confer individual rights of action against another individual (known as lacking *horizontal effect*) as distinct to a right of action by an individual against his State (*vertical effect*).

GODLEY v PERRY
[1960] 1 All ER 36

THE FACTS Godley, a boy of six, bought a plastic catapult from Perry, a stationer. Three days later Godley was using it when the plastic part broke and flew into his left eye causing the loss of sight in that eye.

Perry had bought a quantity of these catapults from Burton & Sons, a wholesaler, by sample and Perry's wife had tested the sample, before placing the order, by pulling back the elastic.

THE DECISION Godley could recover damages (£2,500) from Perry because:

(a) The catapult was not of merchantable quality (section 14(2) of the Sale of Goods Act 1893).
(b) The catapult was not fit for its purpose (section 14(3) of the Sale of Goods Act 1893).

Furthermore, Perry could recover damages from Burton & Sons since the defect in the goods could not have been discovered by a reasonable examination of the sample (section 15(2)(c) of the Sale of Goods Act 1893). Edmund Davies J commented:

In my judgment, to pull back the elastic as the retailer did ... was all that could reasonably be expected of any potential customer, and such an examination wholly failed to make apparent to him, or even to render him alive to the possibility of, such a defect as undoubtedly existed in the accident catapult.

COMMENTARY The most famous explanation of samples by a judge is that of Lord MacNaughten in *Drummond v Van Ingen:*

The office of a sample is to present to the eye the real meaning and intention of the parties with regard to the subject matter of the contract which, owing to the imperfections of language, it may be difficult or impossible to express in words. The sample speaks for itself.

Note: the Sale and Supply of Goods Act 1994, which came into effect on 3 January 1995, reforms the terminology of the Sale of Goods Act 1979 (formerly the Sale of Goods Act 1893). It replaces the expression 'merchantable quality' with 'satisfactory quality'. The change is intended to explain more clearly that the implied condition as to quality covers all aspects of the goods, including both aesthetic aspects (e.g., appearance and finish) and functional aspects (e.g., safety and durability).

GOUGH v THORNE
[1966] 3 All ER 398

THE FACTS On 13 June 1962 Elizabeth Gough, then aged 13, and her brothers, Malcolm, 17 and John, 10, were waiting to cross the New King's Road in south west London. A lorry turning into the New King's Road from Wandsworth Bridge Road stopped, the driver put out his right arm to signal to traffic behind the lorry and then the driver beckoned the children to cross the road in front of the lorry. As the children were crossing the road a car, driven by Mr Thorne, overtook the stationary lorry on its offside and struck Elizabeth who sustaind serious injuries.

Elizabeth, through a 'next friend' claimed damages from Mr Thorne for negligent driving.

At first instance the driver of the car was found to have been going too fast and should have seen the signal given by the lorry driver, so was liable in negligence. However, the judge also held that Elizabeth was careless in advancing past the front of the lorry without pausing to see if any vehicle was coming past the lorry on its offside. Accordingly, the judge held that there was contributory negligence by Elizabeth which he assessed at one-third.

There was an appeal to the Court of Appeal against the finding of contributory negligence.

THE DECISION The finding of contributory negligence was set aside. In the words of Denning MR:

> ... Here she (Elizabeth) was with her elder brother crossing a road. They had been beckoned on by the lorry driver. What more could you expect the child to do than to cross in pursuance of the beckoning ...?
> ... A child has not the road sense or the experience of his or her elders ...

COMMENTARY There is considerable doubt about the age at which persons under 18 can be held liable for contributory negligence. The test seems to be, what would any ordinary child of the age in question do in the same circumstances?

GRIFFITHS v PETER CONWAY
[1939] 1 All ER 685

THE FACTS The plaintiff purchased a tweed coat which had been specially made for her. Shortly after she began to wear the coat she suffered dermatitis (a skin complaint). She brought an action against the seller claiming breach of section 14(3) of the Sale of Goods Act 1893.

THE DECISION There was nothing in the coat that would have affected anyone with a normal skin. Since the plaintiff's skin abnormality had not been made known to the seller the seller was not liable.

COMMENTARY Section 14(3) of the Sale of Goods Act 1893 states that:

> where the seller sells goods in the course of a business and the buyer expressly or by implication makes known to the seller any particular purpose for which the goods are being bought, there is an implied condition that the goods are reasonably fit for that purpose.

Mrs Griffiths failed in her action since she did not expressly make known the particular purpose for which the goods were bought, e.g., by saying 'I have a particularly sensitive skin and require a coat that will not cause an adverse reaction'. Retailers are not expected to be mind readers! On the other hand, if the purpose is obvious, it is not necessary to point the purpose out, e.g., when purchasing a hot water bottle.

Note: the provisions of the Sale of Goods Act 1893 were consolidated into the Sale of Goods Act 1979. Reference should now be to sections of the 1979 Act. Conveniently, most of the section numbers of the 1979 Act correspond to those of the 1893 Act.

HADLEY v BAXENDALE
(1854) 9 Ex 341

THE FACTS The crankshaft of the plaintiff's mill broke. He employed the defendant, a carrier, to take it to a manufacturer to copy it and make a new one. The defendant took longer than necessary to return the new crankshaft, during which time the mill was idle.

The plaintiff sued for loss of profits.

THE DECISION The loss was 'too remote', i.e., the defendant was not liable for he could not reasonably have foreseen the loss, as it was usual for a mill owner to have a spare crankshaft. The plaintiff had not informed the defendant that there was any urgency.

COMMENTARY A plaintiff cannot recover *all* losses arising from a breach of contract. Only those losses which are attributable to the breach are recoverable. Any other loss is said to be 'too remote'.

This case established the principles which are applied to determine whether or not a loss is recoverable. A plaintiff can recover damages for a loss that either:

(a) arises naturally from the breach (it did not in the *Hadley* case, for a mill owner would usually have a spare crankshaft); *or*

(b) ought reasonably to have been in the contemplation of both parties as the likely result of the breach (it was not in the *Hadley* case, as the mill owner did not explain the urgency of the situation).

Losses which fall into neither category are 'too remote' and damages cannot be recovered.

A good illustration of the application of this rule is shown in the case *Victoria Laundry (Windsor) Ltd v Newman Industries Ltd* (see p. 200).

HALL v BROOKLANDS AUTO-RACING CLUB
[1933] 1 KB 205

THE FACTS The plaintiff, a spectator, was injured after two cars collided on the race track, causing one of them to crash through the railings. Two other spectators were killed. It was the first accident of its kind for 23 years.

The plaintiff sued in the tort of negligence.

THE DECISION The defence of *volenti non fit injuria* applied.

The plaintiff was not entitled to damages because this kind of danger to spectators was inherent in the sport and he was taken to have assented to the risk of such an accident.

COMMENTARY *Volenti non fit injuria* is one of the general defences available in an action in tort.

This Latin expression translates as 'no injury can be done to a willing person' or 'he who consents cannot complain'. It means that if a person voluntarily undertakes a task which involves risk, he is generally given to have accepted that risk and so cannot afterwards complain if he is injured — providing the precautions taken by a defendant were adequate in the circumstances. In this particular case the protective iron railings were 4.5 feet from the track and accidents of this type were a rare event.

Note: a spectator does not consent to negligence on the part of participants in a game or sport but 'provided the competition or sport is being performed within the rules and the requirement of the sport and by a person of adequate skill and competence, the spectator does not expect his safety to be regarded by the participant'.

HARRIS v NICKERSON
(1873) 21 WR 635

THE FACTS Nickerson, an auctioneer, advertised in the London newspapers that an auction sale of brewing equipment and office furniture, etc., would be held in Bury St Edmunds on a certain day. Nickerson also issued catalogues listing the various items to be offered for sale. Harris attended the auction sale, intending to bid for items of office furniture, but these lots were withdrawn from the sale.

Harris sued Nickerson for compensation for his loss of time and at first instance was awarded £2 12s 6d (£2.62½ pence). Nickerson appealed.

THE DECISION The Queen's Bench Court held that the advertisements of the auction and the catalogues of the lots did not amount to an offer to sell from which a binding contract with all the persons attending the auction sale could be inferred.

Harris was not entitled to any compensation.

COMMENTARY This case demonstrates the distinction in the law of contract between an offer and a declaration of intention. Whilst an offer is capable of giving rise to a contract upon a valid acceptance, a declaration of intent cannot do so.

It would be impractical for auctioneers to ensure that every person who read their advertisements, etc., received prior notice of the withdrawal of any advertised lot. The conditions of sale used by most auctioneers usually provide that any item advertised for sale can be withdrawn without notice.

HARVEY v FACEY
[1893] AC 552

THE FACTS   The following telegrams were exchanged between the prospective purchaser (the plaintiff) and the owner (the defendant) of a piece of land known as 'Bumper Hall Pen':

'Will you sell us Bumper Hall Pen? Telegraph lowest cash price.'
'Lowest price for Bumper Hall Pen, £900.'
'We agree to buy Bumper Hall Pen for £900 asked by you.'

The owner refused to sell. The prospective purchaser sued, claiming that there was a contract between himself and the owner.

THE DECISION   The second telegram was not an offer but only an indication of what the defendant would accept if he resolved to sell. As it was not an offer, the third telegram could not be an acceptance, i.e., there was no contract between the parties.

COMMENTARY   This case illustrates that an offer must be firm. The courts are reluctant to treat a statement as an offer capable of acceptance unless the statement appears definite.

The second telegram could more accurately be described as a statement of price rather than a definite offer to sell.

Note: the Law of Property (Miscellaneous Provisions) Act 1989 now requires that contracts for the sale of land be in writing.

HEDLEY BYRNE & CO. LTD v HELLER & PARTNERS LTD
[1964] AC 465

THE FACTS The plaintiffs made enquiries concerning the creditworthiness of a company called Easipower, in response to which the defendants (Easipower's bankers) gave favourable references. In reliance on this, the plaintiffs incurred expenditure on Easipower's behalf and, when Easipower went into liquidation, they suffered substantial loss (£17,000).

They sued the defendants in the tort of negligence.

THE DECISION The court of first instance and the Court of Appeal found for the defendants, i.e., decided that they were not liable.

The House of Lords decided that the reference was negligent and wrong and the defendants would have been liable in negligence had the reference not been given 'without responsibility on our part', i.e., the disclaimer protected the defendants so they were not liable.

COMMENTARY This case established that a person could in principle be liable for negligent words (called negligent misstatement) as well as negligent acts. In the event the defendants escaped liability because of a disclaimer of responsibility.

Liability for negligent misstatement arises where:

(a)   the person making the statement has a special knowledge or skill (e.g., a banker);
(b)   he knew the other party relied on these qualities (e.g., an investor);
(c)   the other party suffers a loss as a result of such reliance (e.g., loss of investment).

HENTHORN v FRASER
[1892] 2 Ch 27

THE FACTS   The secretary of a Liverpool land society handed to Henthorn a written offer to sell, for £750, some houses belonging to the society. At about noon the following day the secretary of the society posted to Henthorn a notice withdrawing the offer to sell the houses. This notice was delivered to Henthorn's home in Birkenhead shortly after 5.00 p.m. the same day. Meanwhile Henthorn had posted an acceptance of the offer at 3.50 p.m. some 1 hour 10 minutes before receipt of the notice of revocation of the offer. Henthorn's acceptance was delivered to the offices of the society after they had closed, so it was not read until the next day.

Henthorn sought an order of specific performance to compel the society to complete the sale of the houses to him (the remedy normally given for the breach of a contract for the sale of land — see *Hyde* v *Wrench*, p. 93). At first instance the order for specific performance was refused. Henthorn appealed.

THE DECISION   The Court of Appeal held that where the circumstances are such that it must have been within the contemplation of the parties that, according to the ordinary usages of mankind, the post might be used as a means of communicating the acceptance of an offer, the acceptance is complete as soon as it is posted.

Thus the contract for the sale of the houses was complete on the posting of the acceptance by Henthorn about 1 hour 10 minutes before he received notice of the revocation of the offer (which must be communicated to be effective).

Henthorn was entitled to an order for specific performance.

COMMENTARY   This decision follows an earlier one by the House of Lords that where the parties chose the post to communicate offer and acceptance, any acceptance is binding on posting ('the postal rule'). This rule is one of convenience, and if the offeror does not wish to be bound without immediate notice he can specify in his offer that he will require actual notice of acceptance if postal communication is used. Alternatively the offeror can specify some instant form of communication. Thus the offeror can avoid the problems of the postal rule if he wishes.

HOUSEHOLD FIRE INSURANCE CO. v GRANT
(1879) 27 WR 858

THE FACTS Grant made an application to purchase 100 shares at £1 each in the Household Fire Insurance Co. and paid a deposit of 1 shilling per share to the company's bankers. Grant also agreed to pay the balance of the cost of the shares (19 shillings per share) within 12 months of the date of the allotment of shares to him.

The secretary of the Household Fire Insurance Co. made out a letter of allotment and posted it to Grant. Grant never received the letter of allotment. Later Grant was asked to pay the balance of the cost of his shares but he refused to do so.

THE DECISION Both at first instance and on appeal to the Court of Appeal it was held that Grant was a shareholder and liable to pay for the balance of the cost of his shares. The contract between Grant and the Household Fire Insurance Co., for the purchase of the shares became binding the moment the acceptance of Grant's offer was posted by the secretary to the company.

COMMENTARY This case illustrates the 'postal rule' in the law of contract — a posted acceptance binds on posting even if never received. As was pointed out in the Court of Appeal, if a person making an offer requires *actual* communication of any acceptance of his offer, he is entitled to make this a condition of his offer or alternatively to specify in his offer a means of communication for any acceptance that is more certain than the ordinary post, for example recorded delivery, telex, etc.

HOWARD v SHIRLSTAR CONTAINER TRANSPORT LTD
[1990] 3 All ER 386

THE FACTS   Shirlstar hired out two aircraft for use in Nigeria and when the hire charges became overdue they were entitled under the terms of the hire contract to repossess the aircraft. Shirlstar contracted with Mr Howard, a qualified pilot, to go to Nigeria and recover their aircraft. The contract provided for payments of £25,000 to Mr Howard 'for successfully removing each aircraft from Nigerian airspace', £12,500 to be paid upon notification that an aircraft had been taken out of Nigerian airspace and £12,500 to be paid one month later.

Mr Howard and a radio operator went to Lagos and located one of the aircraft. After a few days Mr Howard was advised by the Nigerian Civil Aviation Department to leave Nigeria as his life and that of his radio operator were in imminent danger. Acting on this advice Mr Howard took possession of the located aircraft and flew it to the Ivory Coast without first obtaining air traffic control clearance, in contravention of Nigerian law.

Mr Howard notified Shirlstar that one aircraft had been removed from Nigeria and they paid the £12,500. However, the Ivory Coast government detained the aircraft and returned it to Nigeria but permitted Mr Howard and his radio operator to return home. Shirlstar refused to pay the second £12,500 so Mr Howard sued for the payment. Shirlstar counterclaimed for the return of the first £12,500.

At first instance Mr Howard was awarded the second £12,500 so Shirlstar appealed to the Court of Appeal.

THE DECISION   The Court of Appeal had to decide what was the meaning of the word 'successfully' in the contract. It was held that in this context the word 'successfully' meant, at most, a flight out of Nigeria without mishap and which ended in a safe landing.

For Shirlstar it was contended that as the performance of the contract involved unlawful actions (breaking Nigerian law) it was not enforceable.

The Court of Appeal held that whilst a contracting party could not normally enforce a contract involving illegality on his part, in this case the unlawful conduct

HOWARD v SHIRLSTAR CONTAINER TRANSPORT LTD — *continued*

was designed to free Mr Howard and his radio operator from immediate danger, so that it would not be an affront to the public conscience to hold that the contract was enforceable and the plaintiff was entitled to the full amount of £25,000.

COMMENTARY This case illustrates the need for all contracts to be drawn in very precise terms, hence the 'small print' in many contracts. Students ought to consider if the decision opens up a loophole in the principle that illegal contracts cannot be enforced.

HYDE v HYDE
(1861–73) All ER Rep 175

THE FACTS As the name suggests, this was a case in family law involving a husband and wife.

THE DECISION This case is not remarkable for the decision but for a description given by Lord Penzance which is generally accepted as the definition of marriage, namely:

> The voluntary union for life of one man and one woman to the exclusion of all others.

COMMENTARY It follows from the definition that:

(a) Forcible marriage and marriage by deceit or mistake are void, i.e., are of no legal effect.

(b) Marriages celebrated under English law are monogamous — 'one man and one woman'. Polygamous marriages, e.g., where a man marries more than one woman, may be recognised under English law but only if they fulfilled the laws of the country in which the marriage was celebrated.

(c) English law does not recognise marriage between persons of the same sex.

(d) The parties commence the marriage with the intention that it should be 'for life'. A divorce does, however, terminate the marriage and the parties are then free to remarry. A judicial separation does not terminate the marriage but terminates the duty to cohabit as man and wife.

(e) Adultery violates the definition — 'to the exclusion of all others'. It is therefore one of the five facts that will support a petition for divorce.

Note: refer to the case of *Corbett* v *Corbett* p. 54, regarding marriage between persons of the same sex.

HYDE v WRENCH
(1840) 49 ER 132

THE FACTS Wrench wrote to Hyde offering to sell his farm to Hyde for £1,000. Agents acting on behalf of Hyde called on Wrench and said that Hyde would be willing to purchase the farm for £950. Wrench said that he wished to consider the matter for a few days. Subsequently Wrench wrote to Hyde saying that he was not prepared to sell the farm for £950. Two days later Hyde wrote saying he 'accepted' the offer by Wrench to sell the farm for £1,000 but Wrench had not renewed his offer. Hyde then brought an action for an order of specific performance (an order to carry out a contract); Wrench contested the action.

THE DECISION No contract existed between the parties for the sale of the farm.

The offer by Hyde of £950 amounted, in law, to a rejection of the offer by Wrench to sell the farm for £1,000 and it was not open to Hyde to accept the original offer by Wrench after rejection.

There being no contract between the parties for the sale of the farm, no order of specific performance could be made.

COMMENTARY This old case remains the authority for the proposition that a counter-offer terminates an original offer and if the original offeror does not wish to renew the offer he need not do so; also that to be effective the acceptance of an offer must be unconditional.

The concept that a contract is a bargain is reflected in this decision. The risk of 'haggling' over the contract price or other terms of the contract is clear; if the 'haggle' does not come off the 'haggler' risks losing the deal, as the original offeror need not renew his offer if he does not want to do so.

JAMES v EASTLEIGH BOROUGH COUNCIL
[1990] 2 All ER 607

THE FACTS The plaintiff and his wife, who were both aged 61, visited a public swimming pool run by the defendant council. The council provided free swimming facilities for persons of 'pensionable age', i.e., women over 60 were admitted free while men were not admitted free until they were 65. The plaintiff was therefore charged 75p while his wife was admitted free. The plaintiff brought an action against the council, claiming that it had unlawfully discriminated against him on the grounds of sex, contrary to section 29 of the Sex Discrimination Act 1975, because the refusal to provide him with free swimming while providing it for his wife amounted to less favourable treatment and therefore discrimination under section 1(1)(a) of that Act.

The county court rejected his claim and the plaintiff's appeal to the Court of Appeal was dismissed, so he sought and obtained leave to appeal to the House of Lords.

THE DECISION The statutory pensionable age of 60 for women and 65 for men was a gender based criterion which directly discriminated between men and women. It followed that the shorthand expression 'pensionable age' likewise discriminated against men, i.e., it treated women more favourably than men. It therefore came within section 1(1)(a) of the Sex Discrimination Act 1975 and so the plaintiff's appeal was allowed.

COMMENTARY Lord Bridge of Harwich observed:

> At first glance this may seem to be a very trivial matter, but the truth is contrary. The phrase 'pensionable age' ... not only governs the age at which persons can qualify for their state pensions but it is also used as the basis on which men and women qualify for a variety of concessions to the elderly, such as free or reduced travel and free prescriptions under the National Health Service.

Note: it was irrelevant that the motive for the discriminatory act was benign, i.e., it made no difference that the purpose of the concession was to provide a free or cheap facility for 'senior citizens'.

RE JONES
[1981] Fam 7

THE FACTS Jones was a soldier serving in Northern Ireland. He had made a formal will leaving his property to his mother. In 1978 he was shot and on the way to hospital, and in the presence of two officers, said, 'If I do not make it, make sure Anne gets all my stuff'. Anne was his fiancée. Jones died the following day.

The court had to decide whether the statement constituted a valid informal will, replacing the earlier will in favour of his mother.

THE DECISION The statement was accepted as his last will.

COMMENTARY Under normal conditions, a will must be in writing, signed by the testator (the person making the will) and witnessed by at least two persons. In certain emergencies or in wartime, however, it is not always possible to comply with the strict rules for making a will, e.g., witnesses may not be available.

The law therefore grants special privileges to soldiers, sailors and airmen on active military service and to sailors at sea. An informal or 'nuncupative' will may be made by such persons, provided they have reached the age of 14. If the will is in writing, no witnesses are needed. If made orally there must be someone present who can later testify as to the deceased's wishes. This is what happened in the above case.

Note: an informal will remains valid even after the hostilities or emergency has ended and after the testator has left the armed forces or ceased to be a sailor.

RE K (DECEASED)
[1985] 1 All ER 403

THE FACTS Mr and Mrs K were married in 1974 and Mrs K had been subjected to considerable matrimonial violence but continued to live with her husband. In September 1982 Mr K was killed by the discharge of a shotgun held by his wife, who was convicted of manslaughter and placed on probation.

In his will Mr K had left the residue of his estate worth about £400,000 to Mrs K for her life and then to four other persons (residuary legatees, i.e., persons entitled to share the remainder of an estate after all the bequests have been satisfied). The residuary legatees objected to Mrs K taking her life interest on the grounds that she should not benefit from her criminal act. Mrs K contended that the Forfeiture Act 1982, which became law two weeks after she killed her husband, had retrospective effect, so that a court now had a discretion whether or not to allow her to benefit by her late husband's will.

The executor of K's will applied to the Chancery Division of the High Court for a determination.

THE DECISION It was held that Mrs K had been a loyal wife who had suffered grave violence and it would be unjust to prevent her taking the benefits her late husband had conferred upon her. Accordingly, Mrs K would be allowed to take her life interest.

COMMENTARY This was the first case involving the provisions of the 1982 Forfeiture Act. Before 1982 the forfeiture rule was based on public policy (the interests of the community). The rule was that a person who had unlawfully killed should not benefit from the act. As in many matrimonial disputes, the violence in *Re K* was not entirely one-sided and the effect of the 1982 Act is to require the court to form a view of the moral culpability of the parties before the exercise of the statutory discretion to set aside the rule.

KELSEN v IMPERIAL TOBACCO CO. LTD

[1957] 2 All ER 343

THE FACTS Mr Kelsen rented a tobacconist's shop and Imperial Tobacco Co. had an advertising sign attached to the wall of the adjoining property so that the sign projected about eight inches into the airspace above Mr Kelsen's shop. The only access to the sign was from Mr Kelsen's premises and he had allowed employees of Imperial Tobacco Co. entry from time to time for cleaning and repair of the sign.

After a business dispute between the parties Mr Kelsen gave Imperial Tobacco Co. notice to remove the sign in so far as it invaded his airspace, subsequently taking an action in trespass for an injunction to require the removal of the sign from his airspace.

THE DECISION The court had first to decide if the lease of the shop to Mr Kelsen included the airspace above. The judge found 'nothing in the lease which displaces the prima facie conclusion which one would otherwise reach that the airspace above the demised premises is a part of the premises conveyed'. (Demised means leased.)

Consequently, in law, Mr Kelsen as the 'tenant' of the airspace above the shop had the right to exclude others and an injunction would be granted to require the portion of the sign projecting into Mr Kelsen's airspace to be removed within 28 days.

COMMENTARY Whilst the motive for the action may be open to some doubt, the decision provides authority for treating an invasion of the airspace immediately above a property as though it were an invasion of the property itself, notwithstanding that there is no damage to the interests of the occupier of the property.

This sort of minor invasion of an airspace can happen when a roof gutter overhangs a boundary, but it may be wise to suffer the trespass rather than the rain-water.

For trespass to airspace refer also to *Baron Bernstein of Leigh* v *Skyviews & General Ltd* (p. 30).

KING v PHILLIPS
[1953] 1 All ER 617

THE FACTS Mrs King was looking out of an upstairs window towards the street when she heard a scream and saw Phillips' taxicab reversing over her child's tricycle but the child could not be seen. As Mrs King was running into the street she met her child, who was unharmed. Mrs King claimed compensation for the nervous shock she had suffered due to the negligence of the taxicab driver, Mr Phillips.

At first instance Mrs King lost her claim for compensation. She appealed.

THE DECISION The Court of Appeal held that in the law of negligence the extent of the duty of care not to cause harm was limited by the test of the foreseeability of the harm and that this included harm caused by nervous shock.

No reasonable driver, even if driving in a manner that caused damage to property, would have anticipated the harm suffered by Mrs King.

Refusal of claim for compensation was upheld.

COMMENTARY The decision in this case followed the decision in *Bourhill* v *Young* (p. 36).

It should be noted that what Mr Phillips could have foreseen is not the test, which is an objective one, namely, what could any reasonabe driver in those circumsances have foreseen.

One problem with claims for nervous shock is that the claimant may be some distance away from the occurrence. For example, if a person on a ladder picking apples from his tree is startled by, say, the sound of a collision between two cars and suffers a nervous shock causing him to drop the apples, ought this to be a sufficient basis to found a claim against the negligent driver of one of the crashed cars?

Note: see the case of *Alcock* v *Chief Constable of South Yorkshire* regarding proximity tests for nervous shock claims (p. 21–2).

KRELL v HENRY

[1903] 2 KB 740

THE FACTS In June 1902 Henry saw an advertisement that a flat (56A Pall Mall), with windows overlooking the route of the forthcoming coronation procession of King Edward VII on 26 and 27 June, was to let for those two days. Henry agreed, in writing, to pay £75 rent for the use of the flat on those two days and paid a deposit of £25 in advance, the balance of the rent being due for payment on 24 June.

On 24 June the coronation of the King was cancelled due to his illness. Henry refused to pay the balance of the agreed rent for the flat, so Krell sued for this sum. At first instance the claim by Krell failed. He appealed.

THE DECISION The Court of Appeal held that the purpose of the agreement for the use of the flat, namely the viewing of the coronation procession on 26 and 27 June, failed without either party being at fault. Although this purpose was not mentioned in the agreement between the parties, it must have been in their contemplation at the time of contracting.

Henry was not liable for the balance of the agreed rent. (Henry did not pursue a claim for the return of his £25 deposit.)

COMMENTARY This case, one of the 'coronation cases', raises the question, 'What did Henry buy — rooms with a view of a coronation procession, or merely rooms with a view?' Had the possibility of cancellation of the coronation been fully considered before the parties contracted, might not Krell have said, 'The hirer must take the risk, I cannot guarantee that the coronation procession will take place or even pass my premises'. The Law Reform (Frustrated Contracts) Act 1943 now regulates situations such as occurred in this case.

LAMPLEIGH v BRAITHWAIT
(1615) Hob 105

THE FACTS   The defendant was convicted of murder and requested the plaintiff to do all he could to get a pardon for him from the king. The plaintiff did so successfully, whereupon he was promised £100 by the reprieved man (the defendant). The money was never paid, so the plaintiff sued on the basis that the defendant was legally obliged to pay. The outcome depended on whether the service provided by the plaintiff amounted to valid consideration.

THE DECISION   The plaintiff was entitled to the £100.
He had provided consideration by 'journeying to and from London and Newmarket' at his own expense and this consideration was valid as the services were performed in response to the defendant's request.

COMMENTARY   The general rule is that consideration must not be 'past' — 'past consideration is no consideration'. This means that an act performed in the past is not consideration for a promise made in the present, e.g., suppose A repairs B's car as a favour after which B promises A £20 for his trouble. If the money is not paid, A cannot obtain it as what he did (repair B's car) was past at the time B promised to pay and past consideration is no consideration. It can be represented as follows:

> A repairs B's car (past consideration) ... after which ... B promises A £20.

Lampleigh v *Braithwait* is an exception to the general rule that past consideration is no consideration. The distinguishing feature is that the defendant *requested* the service. The court considered that the request implied that the service would ultimately be paid for — the previous request and the subsequent promise to pay for it were treated as part of the same transaction. It can be represented as follows:

1. Request to obtain pardon
2. Lampleigh obtains pardon
3. Braithwait promises £100

The promise to pay 'attaches' to the request, therefore the obtaining of the pardon is not 'past'.

LEAF v INTERNATIONAL GALLERIES
[1950] 2 KB 86

THE FACTS   In 1944 the plaintiff bought a picture from the defendants which they both honestly believed had been painted by the artist Constable. In 1949 the plaintiff discoverd that it was not a genuine Constable and he claimed rescission on the ground of innocent misrepresentation.

THE DECISION   The plaintiff's action failed. There had been an innocent misrepresentation but the lapse of five years (1944–1949) was sufficient to bar the plaintiff's right of rescission — even though he had not previousy discovered the misrepresentation.

COMMENTARY   A misrepresentation is a false statement of fact that induces a contract. An innocent misrepresentation occurs where the false statement has been made in the honest belief that the statement is true — as in this case.

The party misled can bring an action for rescission. This amounts to a request that the parties be restored to their original positions (i.e., pre-contractual).

However, it is a discretionary remedy and the court may refuse to grant it if there is a long time delay between the innocent misrepresentation and the application of rescission — as here. 'It behoves the purchaser either to verify or, as the case may be, to disprove the representation within a reasonable time, or else stand or fall by it.'

Note: the court considered the legal effect of the mistake that had occurred concerning the subject-matter of the contract (the painting), but decided that it amounted to a mistake 'as to quality' and this was insufficient to render the contract void.

'it was not a genuine Constable'

LEWIS v AVERAY
[1971] 3 All ER 907

THE FACTS Lewis advertised his car for sale and a man who answered the advertisement agreed to buy the car for £450. The purchaser said he was Richard Green the actor and offered Lewis a cheque in payment for the car which was signed 'R. A. Green'. The purchaser wanted to take the car away at once and Lewis asked for some proof that the purchaser was R. A. Green, the actor. The purchaser produced a film studio pass in the name of 'Richard A. Green' which carried a photograph of the purchaser. Lewis, after inspecting this evidence of identity allowed the car to be taken away at once in exchange for the cheque.

The car was sold by 'Green' to Averay without delay for cash, and when Lewis found the cheque he had accepted in payment for his car was dishonoured he traced the car to Averay and claimed it back. The man representing himself as 'Richard Green' had vanished (with, of course, Averay's cash).

THE DECISION Where a transaction takes place between persons who are 'face to face' there is a presumption that the offer by one person (in this case Lewis) is made to the other person and not to any person that other person claims to be, unless it is clear from the negotiations leading up to the transaction that the transaction is only to be with the represented person and no one else. Thus Lewis offered to sell his car to an unknown person (a rogue) and not Richard Green. Consequently the rogue obtained a good title to the car until Lewis sought to avoid the transaction for non-payment, by which time the rogue had passed his title in this car to Averay.

The car was thus the legal property of Averay. The claim by Lewis failed.

COMMENTARY The presumption of dealing with the person actually present and not who that person claims to be can be rebutted if it is made very clear in the negotiations that the deal is with and only with the represented person. Merely checking a film studio pass is clearly not sufficient. Rogues come prepared with this

103

type of identity 'evidence' to match the stolen cheque book they want to use. Perhaps it is safer never to sell to strangers for a cheque.

LIMPUS v LONDON GENERAL OMNIBUS CO.
(1862) 1 H & C 526

THE FACTS A bus driver obstructed the plaintiff's bus, causing a collision which damaged it. He had received specific printed instructions not to obstruct other buses. The plaintiffs sued the bus driver's employer, claiming they were vicariously liable for the damage.

THE DECISION The defendants were vicariously liable, for the driver was doing what he was employed to do and it made no difference that he was doing it in a way he was told not to.

COMMENTARY The term 'vicarious liability' is used to describe the situation where one person is liable for the wrongdoings of another. For an employer to be vicariously liable for the torts of his employee it must be shown that the employee was acting 'in the course of his employment'. An employee is within the course of his employment if he is doing what he was employed to do — even if he is doing it improperly or in a way which was forbidden.

The employer will not be liable if the employee is acting outside the course of his employment, e.g., if he is on 'a frolic of his own', such as taking a detour whilst on company business to visit a friend.

Note: in 1900 the defendants were involved in another case which can be contrasted with the above (see *Beard v London General Omnibus Co.*, p. 28).

LOMBARD TRICITY FINANCE LTD v PATON
[1989] 1 All ER 918

THE FACTS In 1985 Mr Paton borrowed the sum of £218 from Lombard Tricity to finance the purchase of a computer from Currys Ltd. The loan was the subject of a credit agreement regulated by the Consumer Credit Act 1974.

One of the terms of the agreement was:

> If the sum payable monthly by me is paid by banker's Direct Debit Mandate, I shall pay an interest charge of 2.3% per month (Annual Percentage Rate 31.3%) or such other percentage as may from time to time be notified to me by you ... If such sum is paid in any other way, I shall pay an interest charge of 2.7% per month (Annual Percentage Rate 37.6%) or such other percentage as may from time to time be notified to me by you ...

The box on the front of the credit agreement setting out the interest rates also stated:

> Interest is payable on credit balance. Subject to variation by the creditor from time to time on notification as required by law.

In March 1986, Lombard Tricity increased their interest charges to 2.45%, for direct debit payments, and to 2.95%, for other payments. Mr Paton then ceased making monthly payments by direct debit so Lombard Tricity applied the higher rate of interest to the outstanding balance of the loan. After making a further four payments (not by direct debit), Mr Paton ceased all payments and Lombard Tricity took a county court action for recovery of the debt.

The county court judge dismissed the claim by Lombard Tricity on the grounds that the credit agreement did not comply with the Consumer Credit (Agreements) Regulations 1983, since the agreement did not specify the circumstances in which a change in the rate of interest charged could occur. Accordingly, the credit agreement was not properly executed as required by the Consumer Credit Act 1974, and thus not enforceable. Lombard Tricity appealed to the Court of Appeal.

LOMBARD TRICITY FINANCE LTD v PATON
— continued

THE DECISION The Court of Appeal held that a credit agreement could provide for the lender to unilaterally vary the rate of interest charged on a loan subject to notice to the borrower. The reference in the 1983 Regulations to 'the circumstances in which any variation ... may occur' did not mean circumstances such as changes in market rates of interest.

The credit agreement did not infringe the 1983 Regulations or consequently, the Consumer Credit Act 1974, and was an enforceable agreement. Lombard Tricity was awarded £192.75.

COMMENTARY It appears that not only has a lender the contractual right to vary, upon notice, his interest rate but is under no legal obligation to set out in the agreement the circumstances which might cause a change in interest rates.

MAHON v OSBORNE
[1939] 2 KB 14

THE FACTS A swab was found in the plaintiff's body during an operation. It had been left there by the defendant (a surgeon) following a previous operation.

THE DECISION The defendant was liable in the tort of negligence.

COMMENTARY This case is used to illustrate the application of the latin maxim *res ipsa loquitur* (the thing speaks for itself).

The maxim applies to situations where the inference of negligence is irresistible, i.e., the accident in question is one which would not ordinarily occur unless those in charge failed to exercise proper care, e.g., where two trains collide on the same railway line.

If the plaintiff successfuly raises the plea of *res ipsa loquitur*, the burden of proof switches to the defendant to prove he was not negligent. Lord Denning in another case illustrated it as follows:

> A plaintiff is entitled to say, 'I went into hospital to be cured of two stiff fingers, and my hand is useless. That should not have happened if due care had been used. Explain it, if you can'.

Unless the defendant can exonerate himself, the plaintiff is entitled to judgment. The defendant will be exonerated if he shows how the accident actually occurred and if this true explanation is consistent with due care on his part. Alternatively, he may prove that there was no lack of care on his part or on the part of anyone for whom he is responsible.

Re McARDLE
[1951] 1 All ER 905

THE FACTS In his will McArdle directed that his wife, if she survived him, could live in his house for the remainder of her life (a tenant for life) but then the property was to be shared between his children. After McArdle died his widow lived in the house and spent £488 on alterations and improvements to the property.

When the work had been completed all the children who would eventually inherit the property signed a document which stated: 'In consideration of your carrying out certain alterations and improvements to the property, we hereby agree that the executors shall repay to you from the estate, when distributed, the sum of £488 in settlement of the amount spent on such improvements.'

Subsequently, the executors of McArdle's will refused to pay the £488.

THE DECISION The Court of Appeal held that the document signed by all the children was not a binding contract as Mrs McArdle had not given good consideration for the promise to repay the £488, since at the time of signing the document all the work of alteration and improvement to the house had been completed. Thus the consideration provided by Mrs McArdle for the repayment promise was past consideration.

COMMENTARY This case demonstrates the rule in the law of contract that 'past consideration is no consideration'.

In general, the other party's promise cannot be bought by a promise to do something that has already been done *unless the act has been requested* (see *Lampleigh* v *Braithwait*, p. 100). The McArdle children never asked their mother to spend money on alterations and improvements to what would become their house; Mrs McArdle acted on her own initiative.

McCONNELL v CHIEF CONSTABLE OF GREATER MANCHESTER
[1990] 1 All ER 423

THE FACTS On 21 March 1983, the police were called to a carpet shop in Oldham. On arrival, a police constable found Mr McConnell seated in the office of the shop manager and refusing to leave the premises. The constable escorted Mr McConnell out of the shop, whereupon he attempted to re-enter the shop. The constable then arrested Mr McConnell under his common law powers of having reasonable grounds for suspecting that if Mr McConnell did re-enter the shop a breach of the peace might occur.

After the arrest, Mr McConnell was taken to the local police station and detained until the following day when he appeared before the magistrates' court on a police application that he be bound over to keep the peace (no criminal charges were preferred). The justices refused a binding-over order as they were not satisfied that a re-entry to the shop might reasonably have been expected to lead to a breach of the peace. Subsequently, Mr McConnell sued the Chief Constable, as the employer of the police officer, for damages for false imprisonment.

At first instance the trial judge was asked to rule on a point of law on which there was no authority, namely, at common law could a breach of the peace occur on private premises? The judge held this was possible and Mr McConnell appealed to the Court of Appeal.

THE DECISION As Glidewell LJ put it 'the concept of a breach of the peace is about as old as English law itself' and their Lordships expressed surprise that the point had never been settled. It was held that a breach of the peace could occur on private premises and the ruling of the trial judge was upheld.

COMMENTARY The power vested in the Justices of the Peace to bind over any citizen to keep the peace dates from 1361. That a breach of the peace can occur on private premises is now settled law unless and until either the House of Lords or Parliament see fit to change the decision.

McCONNELL v CHIEF CONSTABLE OF GREATER MANCHESTER — *continued*

Students should consider the question of whether or not a plaintiff in the situation of Mr McConnell could now bring an action for false imprisonment if arrested on 'reasonable suspicion' of an imminent breach of the peace on private premises. 'Reasonable suspicion' has not been clearly defined but the best test is an objective one, namely, would any ordinary person having the same knowledge as the police officer have the same suspicion? In this case if there had been an 'an objective person' present inside and then outside the shop, would they have formed the same view of Mr McConnell's actions as the police officer?

McLEAN v PARIS TRAVEL SERVICE LTD
[1976] IRLR 202

THE FACTS The complainant, who at the time the dispute arose, was a single lady, worked as a reservation ticketing clerk for the defendant company. She intended to marry Mr McLean, who was an assistant manager with the same firm. The company's policy was not to employ married couples 'who worked in close proximity' and so, on the day before her marriage, the defendant was dismissed. She complained to the London Tribunal that her dismissal was unfair (contrary to the Industrial Relations Act 1971), and that she had been discriminated against on grounds of her sex (contrary to the Sex Discrimination Act 1975).

THE DECISION The tribunal found that the 'close proximity' policy of the employer was not a sufficient reason to justify her dismissal and that her dismissal was unfair. She had also been the subject of sex discrimination. She was awarded joint compensation, i.e., under the Industrial Relations Act 1971 and Sex Discrimination Act 1975, of £117 and £200 for 'injury to feelings' under the Sex Discrimination Act 1975.

COMMENTARY Discrimination within the terms of the Sex Discrimination Act 1975 involves treating one person 'less favourably' than another in the same or similar circumstances, intentionally or otherwise, because of his or her sex. Where an act of unlawful discrimination is established, any consequent dismissal is likely to be unfair within the terms of employment protection legislation and proceedings may be brought under both statutes at the same tribunal.

There is now no limit for compensation in discrimination claims. The case of *Marshall* v *Southampton Area Health Authority* [1993] obliged the government to remove the upper limit on compensation.

Note: legislation relating to unfair dismissal was consolidated into the Employment Protection (Consolidation) Act 1978, and references should now be to that Act, as amended. The rules dealing with sex discrimination are contained in the Sex Discrimination Acts

McLEAN v PARIS TRAVEL SERVICE LTD — *continued*

1975–86 (amended by the Employment Protection Act 1989), together with the Equal Pay Act 1970 and regulations thereunder.

McLOUGHLIN v O'BRIAN
[1983] 1 AC 410

THE FACTS Mr McLoughlin and his three children aged 2, 7 and 17 were injured in a road accident caused by the negligence of O'Brian, and they were taken to hospital. A motorist who had seen the accident went to the family home and told Mrs McLoughlin what had happened, afterwards taking her to the hospital. On arrival at the hospital Mrs McLoughlin was told that her daughter, aged 2, had died of her injuries and she saw her injured husband and other children before they had received any treatment. As a result Mrs McLoughlin suffered severe and persisting nervous shock and claimed compensation from the negligent driver.

At first instance the claim was rejected on the grounds that Mrs McLoughlin's nervous shock was not reasonably foreseeable. On appeal the claim was also rejected on the grounds that a duty of care could only be imposed in relation to persons who were in close proximity to the negligent act, notwithstanding that the injury might be reasonably foreseeable. Mrs McLoughlin further appealed to the House of Lords.

THE DECISION The test of liability for nervous shock was the reasonable foreseeability of the injury happening as a result of negligence. Accordingly Mrs McLoughlin was entitled to compensation; the fact that she was not at or near the scene of the road accident was not material.

COMMENTARY This decision by the House of Lords is of considerable significance and may indicate a change in judicial attitudes towards claims for nervous shock arising as a result of negligence. The facts raise the question of possible liability by the hospital in allowing a close relative to see untreated, badly injured persons which it could be said is almost certain to cause nervous shock to that relative.

Note: the arbitrators for nervous shock claims by survivors of the *Herald of Free Enterprise* accident in 1987 have ruled that to qualify for compensation a nervous shock must give rise to a recognised psychiatric illness such as Post Traumatic Stress Disorder (PTSD) or 'pathological' grief. This decision *must* be read in conjunction with the later decision in *Alcock* v *Chief Constable of South Yorkshire* (p. 21–2).

MERRITT v MERRITT
[1970] 2 All ER 760

THE FACTS Mr Merritt left the matrimonial home which he jointly owned with Mrs Merritt subject to a building society mortgage. Later, the parties had a meeting in Mr Merritt's car during which he agreed to pay Mrs Merritt £40 per month on condition that she paid the mortgage repayments out of this sum. Mrs Merritt refused to leave the car until the agreement was recorded in writing, so Mr Merritt wrote out the following statement and signed it: 'In consideration of the fact that you will pay all charges in connection with the house until such time as the mortgage repayment has been completed I will agree to transfer the property into your sole ownership.'

After Mrs Merritt had completed all the mortgage repayments Mr Merritt refused to transfer the house to his wife. Mrs Merritt sued on the agreement and the question for the court was whether or not the parties had made a domestic agreement, which would not be binding, or a contract, which could be enforced.

THE DECISION An agreement between a husband and wife is normally a domestic agreement and there is no intention to enter legal relations, i.e., no intention that any promise can be enforced.

Here the parties, although married, were not living in amity and might not rely upon 'honourable understandings', so it was to be assumed that they intended to create legal relations in their agreement; consequently the agreement between Mr and Mrs Merritt was a contract enforceable at law.

COMMENTARY This case vividly illustrates the danger of anyone, married or not, entering into agreements without advice from a solicitor, law centre or citizens advice bureau. If Mr Merritt had not bound himself, the division of the jointly owned property, if decided by a court, might have resulted in a different outcome.

The case can be used to show the essential difference between a domestic agreement and a contract.

MORRIS v MURRAY
The Guardian, 3 August 1990

THE FACTS Mr Morris and Mr Murray spent several hours drinking together then Mr Murray suggested that they go for a trip in his light aircraft. At the airfield, Mr Morris assisted Mr Murray to prepare the aircraft and they took off, with Mr Murray piloting, in very adverse conditions when all other flying had been suspended. Shortly after takeoff, the aircraft crashed and the pilot, Mr Murray, was killed and the passenger, Mr Morris, was badly injured. An autopsy showed that the pilot was more than three times over the legal limit for driving a motor vehicle, having consumed the equivalent of 17 whiskies. Mr Morris sued the personal representatives of Mr Murray for damages in negligence for his injuries.

At first instance Mr Morris was awarded damages of £130,000. The personal representatives of Mr Murray appealed to the Court of Appeal.

THE DECISION The Court of Appeal held that Mr Morris knew:

(a) That he was going on a flight.
(b) That he was going to be piloted by Mr Murray.
(c) That Mr Murray had consumed a large amount of alcohol.
(d) That he was capable of appreciating the risks.

Since Mr Morris knew what he was doing, he knowingly and willingly embarked on a flight with a drunken pilot. Consequently, Mr Morris implicitly waived his rights in the event of injury caused by Mr Murray's failure to fly with reasonable care. The maxim *volenti non fit injuria* applied. The award of damages was set aside.

COMMENTARY The maxim *volenti non fit injuria* means 'he who consents cannot complain' (*Hall* v *Brooklands Auto-racing Club* (p. 83)). A case better illustrating the maxim would be hard to find. As Fox LJ put it:

> ... the wild irresponsibility of the venture was such that the law should not intervene to award damages and should leave the loss where it fell. Flying is dangerous and flying with a drunken pilot is great folly.

MURPHY v BRENTWOOD DISTRICT COUNCIL
[1990] 2 All ER 908

THE FACTS In 1970 Mr Murphy purchased a new semi-detached house, 38, Vineway, Brentwood, from Messrs ABC Homes. The House was one of 160 on a new estate and the site of numbers 36 and 38 was made up ground, so the builders had consulting engineers design special raft foundations. The foundation design was sent to the District Council for approval who had it checked by their consulting engineers before granting approval under the Building Regulations.

In 1981 serious cracks started appearing in the walls which Mr Murphy reported to his insurers. Investigations disclosed that the raft foundation had failed, also that the drainage pipes were cracked and leaking. Subsequently, a gas pipe split due to structural movement. The adjoining house was also affected and repairs to Mr Murphy's house were estimated to cost £45,000, but the two insurance companies could not agree the division of liability.

Accordingly, Mr Murphy decided to sell and obtained £30,000 for the house which, without the defects, had a market value of £65,000.

Mr Murphy claimed against the District Council in negligence and at first instance it was held that there was imminent danger to the safety of the occupants due to the condition of the house. Mr Murphy was awarded £38,777 with interest and costs against the District Council who appealed to the Court of Appeal, which upheld the first instance decision.

The District Council further appealed to the House of Lords.

THE DECISION The House of Lords held that the award would be set aside as the dangerous defect in the foundations had not caused personal injury, death or damage to other property but only economic loss to Mr Murphy, for which the District Council could not be held liable.

Their Lordships decided to exercise the right they adopted in 1966 to change a previous decision of the House of Lords. Thus, the decision in *Anns* v *Merton London Borough* [1977] (that a Council was liable for economic loss due to failure to properly supervise construction) would be reversed.

MURPHY v BRENTWOOD DISTRICT COUNCIL
— *continued*

COMMENTARY   The reason for the change in attitude towards liability for pure economic loss seems to be that a dangerous defect in a building, once known, becomes a defect in quality, and to allow a plaintiff to recover in these circumstances might open the 'floodgates' to claims. No doubt their Lordships had in mind that economic loss caused by building settlement is usually covered by insurance (Mr Murphy had his £35,000 loss repaid by his insurers). Their Lordships also indicated that product liability for buildings should be a matter for Parliament to decide.

NASH v INMAN
[1908] 2 KB 1

THE FACTS   The defendant, a minor, ordered a quantity of clothing (including 11 fancy waistcoats) from the plaintiff, a tailor. When the clothes were delivered the defendant refused to pay the bill of nearly £123. The tailor sued for the money.

THE DECISION   The tailor's action failed. The defendant's father (an architect) showed that his son had plenty of clothes suitable to his standard of living, i.e., the clothes supplied by the tailor were 'non-necessaries', therefore the minor was not obliged to pay.

COMMENTARY   The common law provides that contracts made by minors for necessaries supplied, e.g., food, clothing, housing, transport, are enforceable. On the other hand, contracts with minors for 'non-necessaries' are not enforceable.

This case illustrates that even something as basic as clothing can be a non-necessary if the minor already had an adequate supply of the items concerned. Two questions must therefore be answered:

(a)   Is the article concerned capable of being a necessary? — 'articles of mere luxury are always excluded, though luxurious articles of utility are in some cases allowed'.

(b)   Is the article concerned a necessary in the particular cirucmstances? e.g., if the defendant had been a poor student ordering a warm overcoat it would probably have been a necessary with the result that the student would have to pay!

Note: (i) Where a minor fraudulently obtains goods (e.g., by lying about his age), he may be compelled to return them. (ii) Traders dealing with minors can protect themselves by insisting on a guarantor. The guarantor (usually a parent or guardian) undertakes that, if the minor fails to meet all or any of the payments, he will pay the trader. The Minors Contracts Act 1987 provides that such guarantees are binding even if made in connection with contracts that are unenforceable against the minor, e.g., where the contract is for a 'non-necessary'.

NATIONAL COAL BOARD v EVANS & CO. AND ANOTHER
[1951] 2 KB 861

THE FACTS   Power to the plaintiffs' mine was cut off when an excavator operated on behalf of the defendants cut through an electric cable. The plaintiffs sued in trespass and negligence.

THE DECISION   The defence of inevitable accident applied. The defendants were not liable as neither they nor the landowners knew of the existence of the cable and it was not marked on any available map.

COMMENTARY   Inevitable accident is one of the general defences to an action in tort, i.e., a defence available to a defendant in every action where appropriate. If successful, it justifies or excuses the defendant's action and he is not liable.

Inevitable accident refers to the situation where something happens which could not have been avoided by taking ordinary precautions, i.e., the precautions a reasonable man could be expected to take. A reasonable man is not expected to guard against every eventuality — 'People must guard against reasonable probabilities but they are not bound to guard against fantastic possibilities'.

Cases involving inevitable accident are rare. Generally the burden of proof is already on the plaintiff, e.g., in negligence the plaintiff must establish the defendant's lack of care. If he cannot do so, the defendant is not liable.

Thus in *Stanley* v *Powell*, another case used to illustrate inevitable accident, the defendant was not liable for injury to the plaintiff which occurred during a shoot when one of the defendant's shots glanced off the bough of a tree and struck the plaintiff. The court considered the defendant had not been negligent and that the injury was inflicted accidentally.

NICHOLS v MARSLAND
(1876) 2 Ex D 1

THE FACTS   For many years Miss Marsland had had several artificial ornamental lakes on her estate, which had been formed by damming up a natural stream. Following an extraordinary rainfall said to be 'greater and more violent than any within living memory', the walls of the lakes collapsed under the weight of water and the rush of escaping water into the natural stream carried away four bridges over the stream that were the responsibility of Nichols.

Nichols claimed the cost of replacing the bridges from Miss Marsland, who contested liability.

THE DECISION   Miss Marsland was held not to be liable for the loss of the four bridges, which was caused by an extraordinary act of nature that Miss Marsland could not have been expected to anticipate.

COMMENTARY   This decision suggests that a person cannot be liable for situations arising from what are often called 'acts of God'. An 'act of God' may be regarded, in law, as a process of nature not due to the act of man. The accepted modern criterion for 'acts of God' is whether or not human foresight and prudence could reasonably recognise the possibility of the particular process or nature occurring.

The correctness of the decision in this case is therefore now open to doubt, for the criterion applied in the case was whether or not the event was reasonably to be anticipated.

Reasonable anticipation of an event is not at all the same thing as prudent foresight of the *possibility* of that event happening. In England it may not be reasonable to anticipate say, a hurricane, but nevertheless it cannot be said that there is no possibility of such an event.

NORDENFELT v MAXIM NORDENFELT GUNS & AMMUNITION CO.

[1894] AC 535

THE FACTS The plaintiff was an inventor and a manufacturer of guns and ammunition. He sold his business and entered into a contract with the defendants agreeing that for a period of 25 years he would not carry on a similar business anywhere in the world.

A dispute arose and the validity of the restraint was brought into question.

THE DECISION Although contracts in restraint of trade are prima facie (at first sight) void, this agreement was reasonable in the circumstances and binding between the parties.

COMMENTARY A contract in restraint of trade is one which restricts a person in the carrying on of his trade or business. Though prima facie void, the courts will enforce them if they are:

(a)   reasonable between the parties;
(b)   reasonable, having regard to the interests of the public.

In this case both conditions were satisfied:

(a)   The plaintiff had been adequately compensated in return for giving up his manufacturing rights.
(b)   The agreement increased exports.

Note: contracts in restraint of trade fall into three categories:

1.   Contracts between the buyer and seller of a business (as above).
2.   Contracts between an employer and employee — restraining an employee from competing with his employer when he leaves (see *Fitch* v *Dewes*, p. 75).
3.   Contracts between traders/distributors regulating conditions of trade, including so called 'solus trading agreements' whereby one party agrees to sell or distribute the goods of one manufacturer only (see *Esso Petroleum* v *Harper's Garages Ltd*, p. 72).

NORWICH & PETERBOROUGH BUILDING SOCIETY v STEED (NO. 2)
[1993] 1 All ER 330

THE FACTS   Mr Steed, the freehold owner of a house which was subject to a local authority mortgage, permitted his mother, his sister and her husband to live in the house while he was living in the United States. His sister and her husband persuaded him to execute a power of attorney in favour of his mother and then either tricked the mother into executing a transfer of the house in their favour under the power of attorney or forged her signature on the transfer. On the same day the sister and her husband borrowed £15,000 from the building society on the security of the property, supposedly to enable them to purchase it for £24,500 from Mr Steed. In fact they paid off the local authority mortgage, amounting to £1,800, and kept the balance. The sister and her husband defaulted on the mortgage and the building society brought an action for possession of the property. Mr Steed claimed that, among other things, he was entitled to rely on a plea of *non est factum* on the ground that the mother did not know that she had been appointed attorney and did not know that she was signing a transfer of the property.

THE DECISION   The plea of *non est factum* had not been established notwithstanding the fact that the mother had apparently been tricked into signing the transfer since either:

(a)   she possessed sufficient understanding but had failed to inform herself on the effect of the transfer before signing it; or
(b)   she lacked sufficient understanding, in which case Mr Steed was not entitled to repudiate the transfer made by her.

Moreover, if Mrs Steed was ignorant of her responsibilities and status as the donee of a power of attorney, her ignorance was attributable to Mr Steed's failure to tell her about it.

COMMENTARY   Taken literally, the doctrine of *non est factum* applies when the person whose name appears

PARKINSON v COLLEGE OF AMBULANCE LTD AND HARRISON
[1925] 2 KB 1

THE FACTS The secretary of the defendant charity fraudulently represented to the plaintiff that the charity was in a position to secure a knighthood for him — if he made an adequate donation. The plaintiff paid £3,000 to the charity but no knighthood was forthcoming, so he sued for the return of his money.

THE DECISION The plaintiff was unable to recover the money as the contract was illegal and void.

COMMENTARY Any contract that tends to promote corruption in public life is illegal and void. A void contract is no contract at all, i.e., it is not legally binding and the parties to it generally have no redress.

Persons in 'public life' in this context include civil servants, judges, army personnel, etc.

So if a civil servant obtained promotion by promising his superior a sum of money, the agreement between them would be illegal and void. Bribery and corruption are not a good basis for securing the interests of the nation; as one writer commented, 'all such contracts must have a material influence to diminish the respectablity, responsibility and purity of public officers and to introduce a system of official patronage, corruption and deceit wholly at war with the public interests'.

Note: although the plaintiff had been deceived into believing that the charity was capable of securing a knighthood, the judge concluded that the plaintiff must have known that the whole arrangement was illegal.

NORWICH & PETERBOROUGH BUILDING SOCIETY v STEED (NO. 2) — *continued*

on it has not, in fact, signed the document. However, it also covers cases in which a person who has signed a document is, nonetheless, allowed to repudiate the document. The factors which must be established for a plea of *non est factum* to succeed are outlined in the case *Saunders* v *Anglia Building Society*. In that case Lord Reid said that the doctrine:

> ... must be kept within narrow limits if it is not to shake the confidence of those who habitually and rightly rely on signatures where there is no obvious reason to doubt their validity ... there must be a heavy burden of proof on the person who seeks to invoke this remedy.

It is perhaps not surprising then that the Court of Appeal dismissed Mr Steed's appeal. As Butler-Sloss LJ pointed out:

> the donor of a power of attorney who appoints as his attorney a person incapable of understanding the import of a simple transfer can hardly be allowed, if the donee signs a transfer without any understanding of what he or she is doing, to repudiate the transfer on the ground of a lack of understanding on the part of the donee.

Note: Mrs Steed died during the course of the case. A handwriting expert was instructed. His report concluded that there was a high probability that Mrs Steed did sign the transfer. From this point on the defence abandoned the forgery allegation.

O'CONNOR v SWAN & EDGAR AND CARMICHAEL
[1963] 107 SJ 215

THE FACTS Mrs O'Connor was employed by Swan & Edgar, the former department store in London, as a sales assistant. Whilst at work in the store Mrs O'Connor was struck and injured by a section of ceiling that fell down.

Mrs O'Connor, being on the premises for a lawful purpose and thus in law a 'visitor', sued Swan & Edgar as occupiers under the provisions of the Occupiers' Liability Act 1957. The Act provides that occupiers shall have a 'common duty of care' to take such care as in all the circumstances of the case is reasonable to see the visitors will be reasonably safe in using the premises for the purposes for which they are invited.

Swan & Edgar together with the ceiling contractor, Carmichael, as co-defendant, sought to rely on the following provision of the 1957 Act:

Where damage is caused to a visitor by a danger due to a faulty execution of any work of construction, maintenance or repair by an independent contractor employed by the occupier, the occupier is not to be treated without more as answerable for the danger if in all the circumstances he had acted reasonably in entrusting the work to an independent contractor and had taken such steps (if any) as he reasonably could in order to satisfy himself that the contractor was competent and that the work had been properly done.

THE DECISION It was held that Carmichael was liable as the occupier's independent competent contractor.

COMMENTARY It is essential to bear in mind that if an occupier is to avoid liability under the 1957 Act for the work of another, then it is up to the occupier to ensure as far as he can that his contractor is competent. Occupiers should have this in mind when having work done on their premises by relatives and friends, etc., which might subsequently injure a visitor.

PARIS v STEPNEY BOROUGH COUNCIL
[1951] 1 All ER 42

THE FACTS In 1942 Paris, who had lost the sight of one eye, took temporary employment with Stepney Council as a garage mechanic. In 1946 Paris was refused permanent and pensionable employment on account of his disability and in 1947 was given notice that his temporary employment was to be terminated. Two days before the notice expired Paris was working under a vehicle when a piece of metal injured his good eye, resulting in the loss of the sight in the good eye with the consequence that Paris became blind.

Paris claimed in negligence on the basis that his employer, Stepney Council, had failed in their duty of care for employee's safety in that the Council had not provided protective eye visors for use by employees and had not required employees to wear such visors.

THE DECISION At first instance Paris was awarded damages but on appeal the Court of Appeal set aside the award of damages, so Paris further appealed to the House of Lords.

By a 3:2 majority the House of Lords held that a careful employer must not merely take account of the degree of risk of injury to employees but must also have regard to the gravity of the consequences of such injury. The award of damages was restored, as the Council ought to have realised, at least from the time permanent employment was refused, that an eye injury to a one-eyed employee might have much more serious consequences than the same eye injury would have for a normally sighted employee.

COMMENTARY The rather unusual facts of this case provided the House of Lords with the opportunity to expand the duty of care in the law of negligence so that the level of the duty will vary with the circumstances.

PEARCE v BROOKS
(1866) 14 WR 614

THE FACTS Pearce was a coach-builder who supplied, on hire, to Brooks a brougham (a closed carriage).
Brooks was a known prostitute. When Brooks failed to
pay the hire charges for the brougham Pearce brought
an action to recover the hire charges.

A jury was asked to decide whether Brooks used the
brougham for the purposes of her trade as a prostitute
and, if so, did Pearce know that this was the purpose for
which the brougham was hired?

THE DECISION It was found that the brougham was
used by Brooks as 'a part of her display to attract men'
and that Pearce was fully aware of that fact. Consequently the contract of hire was void as being for an
immoral purpose. Pearce was unable to recover the hire
charges.

COMMENTARY This case supports the view that contracts for immoral purposes cannot exist as they are
void.

Over the years there has been much speculation
about what was displayed in the brougham to attract
men.

PEPPER v WEBB
[1969] 1 WLR 514

THE FACTS Pepper was employed as head gardener by Major Webb. He worked satisfactorily for three months but then his attitude deteriorated. When asked about the arrangements for the greenhouse during the defendant's absence, Pepper replied, 'I couldn't care less about your bloody greenhouse or your sodding garden', and walked off.

He was dismissed summarily, i.e., on the spot, without being given any notice.

Pepper complained that the dismissal was unfair.

THE DECISION The dismissal was justified.

The plaintiff's conduct and his previous bad behaviour indicated an intention to repudiate the contract of employment.

COMMENTARY The Employment Protection (Consolidation) Act 1978, as amended by the Employment Act 1980, provides that an employee has the right not to be unfairly dismissed. Since the 1980 Act it is for an industrial tribunal to decide whether or not the employer acted reasonably.

Certain types of misconduct justify dismissal. They include insolence, persistent laziness, immorality, dishonesty and drunkenness. The misconduct will justify summary dismissal if it directly interferes with the business of the employer, or the employee's ability to perform his services.

One isolated incident of misconduct will not justify summary dismissal, e.g., in *Wilson* v *Racher* a gardener was dismissed for swearing at his employer on one occasion. This was considered to be an exceptional outburst from an otherwise competent and diligent employee who had been provoked by his employer. Therefore there were no grounds for dismissal.

PHARMACEUTICAL SOCIETY OF GREAT BRITAIN v BOOTS CASH CHEMISTS (SOUTHERN) LTD
[1953] 1 All ER 482

THE FACTS   The defendants were prosecuted for infringing a provision of the Pharmacy and Poisons Act 1933 which made it unlawful to sell any listed poison 'unless the sale is effected under the supervision of a registered pharmacist'.

Their shop was self-service and the customer had selected from the shelves a medicine covered by the Act and had taken it to the cash desk where a registered pharmacist was present.

THE DECISION   The display of articles on the shelves was an invitation to treat. The customer made the offer when he presented the goods for payment and there was no 'sale' until his offer to buy was accepted at the cash desk. Since there was a registered pharmacist at the point of sale no offence had been committed.

COMMENTARY   This is an instance where a principle in the law of contract determined the outcome of the case brought in another branch of law.

It illustrates the point that an invitation to treat is not an offer and cannot be accepted. It is an invitation to the other party to make an offer.

It involves the same principle as the later case, *Fisher v Bell* (p. 74) and, like that case, demonstrates the literal way in which the courts interpret the wording of an Act of Parliament.

PHILLIPS v BROOKS LTD
[1919] 2 KB 243

THE FACTS A man named North went into a jewellers' shop owned by Phillips and selected items of jewellery to a value of £3,000, making out a cheque in payment. When signing the cheque with a false name North said, 'You see who I am, I am Sir George Bullough', and gave an address in St James' Square. Phillips had heard of Sir George Bullough and on checking that the address given by North was the correct one for Sir George Bullough he offered to let North take the jewellery away with him, to which North replied that Phillips had better have the cheque cleared first but as it happened he would like to take a diamond ring away with him as it was for his wife's birthday the next day. Phillips then allowed North to have the ring, valued at £450.

When the cheque for £3,000 was dishonoured North was traced and convicted of obtaining the ring by false pretences but North had immediately pawned the ring for £350 with Brooks Ltd and disposed of the money.

Phillips claimed the return of the ring from Brooks Ltd.

THE DECISION Phillips, in fact, contracted to sell and deliver the ring to the person who came into his shop, who was not Sir George Bullough but a man in the name of North. Hence North obtained good title to the ring until such time as Phillips sought to avoid the contract of sale for non-payment. So North, having pawned the ring before non-payment was discovered by Phillips, could pass a good title to Brooks Ltd, who were entitled to retain the ring if the pledge was not redeemed.

COMMENTARY This case illustrates the presumption in the law of contract that in 'face to face' contracts there is an intention to contract with the person *actually present* and not who the person says he or she is.

The presumption can be set aside, but only if a party makes it absolutely clear that the identity of the other party is to be a condition of contracting.

Shopkeepers are not normally interested in the identity of their customers except as a possible indication of ability to pay. So the mistake by Phillips was about an attribute of his customer (the ability to pay).

on it has not, in fact, signed the document. However, it also covers cases in which a person who has signed a document is, nonetheless, allowed to repudiate the document. The factors which must be established for a plea of *non est factum* to succeed are outlined in the case *Saunders* v *Anglia Building Society*. In that case Lord Reid said that the doctrine:

> ... must be kept within narrow limits if it is not to shake the confidence of those who habitually and rightly rely on signatures where there is no obvious reason to doubt their validity ... there must be a heavy burden of proof on the person who seeks to invoke this remedy.

It is perhaps not surprising then that the Court of Appeal dismissed Mr Steed's appeal. As Butler-Sloss LJ pointed out:

> the donor of a power of attorney who appoints as his attorney a person incapable of understanding the import of a simple transfer can hardly be allowed, if the donee signs a transfer without any understanding of what he or she is doing, to repudiate the transfer on the ground of a lack of understanding on the part of the donee.

Note: Mrs Steed died during the course of the case. A handwriting expert was instructed. His report concluded that there was a high probability that Mrs Steed did sign the transfer. From this point on the defence abandoned the forgery allegation.

O'CONNOR v SWAN & EDGAR AND CARMICHAEL
[1963] 107 SJ 215

THE FACTS Mrs O'Connor was employed by Swan & Edgar, the former department store in London, as a sales assistant. Whilst at work in the store Mrs O'Connor was struck and injured by a section of ceiling that fell down.

Mrs O'Connor, being on the premises for a lawful purpose and thus in law a 'visitor', sued Swan & Edgar as occupiers under the provisions of the Occupiers' Liability Act 1957. The Act provides that occupiers shall have a 'common duty of care' to take such care as in all the circumstances of the case is reasonable to see the visitors will be reasonably safe in using the premises for the purposes for which they are invited.

Swan & Edgar together with the ceiling contractor, Carmichael, as co-defendant, sought to rely on the following provision of the 1957 Act:

> Where damage is caused to a visitor by a danger due to a faulty execution of any work of construction, maintenance or repair by an independent contractor employed by the occupier, the occupier is not to be treated without more as answerable for the danger if in all the circumstances he had acted reasonably in entrusting the work to an independent contractor and had taken such steps (if any) as he reasonably could in order to satisfy himself that the contractor was competent and that the work had been properly done.

THE DECISION It was held that Carmichael was liable as the occupier's independent competent contractor.

COMMENTARY It is essential to bear in mind that if an occupier is to avoid liability under the 1957 Act for the work of another, then it is up to the occupier to ensure as far as he can that his contractor is competent. Occupiers should have this in mind when having work done on their premises by relatives and friends, etc., which might subsequently injure a visitor.

PARIS v STEPNEY BOROUGH COUNCIL
[1951] 1 All ER 42

THE FACTS In 1942 Paris, who had lost the sight of one eye, took temporary employment with Stepney Council as a garage mechanic. In 1946 Paris was refused permanent and pensionable employment on account of his disability and in 1947 was given notice that his temporary employment was to be terminated. Two days before the notice expired Paris was working under a vehicle when a piece of metal injured his good eye, resulting in the loss of the sight in the good eye with the consequence that Paris became blind.

Paris claimed in negligence on the basis that his employer, Stepney Council, had failed in their duty of care for employee's safety in that the Council had not provided protective eye visors for use by employees and had not required employees to wear such visors.

THE DECISION At first instance Paris was awarded damages but on appeal the Court of Appeal set aside the award of damages, so Paris further appealed to the House of Lords.

By a 3:2 majority the House of Lords held that a careful employer must not merely take account of the degree of risk of injury to employees but must also have regard to the gravity of the consequences of such injury. The award of damages was restored, as the Council ought to have realised, at least from the time permanent employment was refused, that an eye injury to a one-eyed employee might have much more serious consequences than the same eye injury would have for a normally sighted employee.

COMMENTARY The rather unusual facts of this case provided the House of Lords with the opportunity to expand the duty of care in the law of negligence so that the level of the duty will vary with the circumstances.

PARKINSON v COLLEGE OF AMBULANCE LTD AND HARRISON
[1925] 2 KB 1

THE FACTS The secretary of the defendant charity fraudulently represented to the plaintiff that the charity was in a position to secure a knighthood for him — if he made an adequate donation. The plaintiff paid £3,000 to the charity but no knighthood was forthcoming, so he sued for the return of his money.

THE DECISION The plaintiff was unable to recover the money as the contract was illegal and void.

COMMENTARY Any contract that tends to promote corruption in public life is illegal and void. A void contract is no contract at all, i.e., it is not legally binding and the parties to it generally have no redress.

Persons in 'public life' in this context include civil servants, judges, army personnel, etc.

So if a civil servant obtained promotion by promising his superior a sum of money, the agreement between them would be illegal and void. Bribery and corruption are not a good basis for securing the interests of the nation; as one writer commented, 'all such contracts must have a material influence to diminish the respectablity, responsibility and purity of public officers and to introduce a system of official patronage, corruption and deceit wholly at war with the public interests'.

Note: although the plaintiff had been deceived into believing that the charity was capable of securing a knighthood, the judge concluded that the plaintiff must have known that the whole arrangement was illegal.

PEARCE v BROOKS
(1866) 14 WR 614

THE FACTS Pearce was a coach-builder who supplied, on hire, to Brooks a brougham (a closed carriage). Brooks was a known prostitute. When Brooks failed to pay the hire charges for the brougham Pearce brought an action to recover the hire charges.

A jury was asked to decide whether Brooks used the brougham for the purposes of her trade as a prostitute and, if so, did Pearce know that this was the purpose for which the brougham was hired?

THE DECISION It was found that the brougham was used by Brooks as 'a part of her display to attract men' and that Pearce was fully aware of that fact. Consequently the contract of hire was void as being for an immoral purpose. Pearce was unable to recover the hire charges.

COMMENTARY This case supports the view that contracts for immoral purposes cannot exist as they are void.

Over the years there has been much speculation about what was displayed in the brougham to attract men.

PEPPER v WEBB
[1969] 1 WLR 514

THE FACTS   Pepper was employed as head gardener by Major Webb. He worked satisfactorily for three months but then his attitude deteriorated. When asked about the arrangements for the greenhouse during the defendant's absence, Pepper replied, 'I couldn't care less about your bloody greenhouse or your sodding garden', and walked off.

He was dismissed summarily, i.e., on the spot, without being given any notice.

Pepper complained that the dismissal was unfair.

THE DECISION   The dismissal was justified.

The plaintiff's conduct and his previous bad behaviour indicated an intention to repudiate the contract of employment.

COMMENTARY   The Employment Protection (Consolidation) Act 1978, as amended by the Employment Act 1980, provides that an employee has the right not to be unfairly dismissed. Since the 1980 Act it is for an industrial tribunal to decide whether or not the employer acted reasonably.

Certain types of misconduct justify dismissal. They include insolence, persistent laziness, immorality, dishonesty and drunkenness. The misconduct will justify summary dismissal if it directly interferes with the business of the employer, or the employee's ability to perform his services.

One isolated incident of misconduct will not justify summary dismissal, e.g., in *Wilson* v *Racher* a gardener was dismissed for swearing at his employer on one occasion. This was considered to be an exceptional outburst from an otherwise competent and diligent employee who had been provoked by his employer. Therefore there were no grounds for dismissal.

PHARMACEUTICAL SOCIETY OF GREAT BRITAIN v BOOTS CASH CHEMISTS (SOUTHERN) LTD
[1953] 1 All ER 482

THE FACTS   The defendants were prosecuted for infringing a provision of the Pharmacy and Poisons Act 1933 which made it unlawful to sell any listed poison 'unless the sale is effected under the supervision of a registered pharmacist'.

Their shop was self-service and the customer had selected from the shelves a medicine covered by the Act and had taken it to the cash desk where a registered pharmacist was present.

THE DECISION   The display of articles on the shelves was an invitation to treat. The customer made the offer when he presented the goods for payment and there was no 'sale' until his offer to buy was accepted at the cash desk. Since there was a registered pharmacist at the point of sale no offence had been committed.

COMMENTARY   This is an instance where a principle in the law of contract determined the outcome of the case brought in another branch of law.

It illustrates the point that an invitation to treat is not an offer and cannot be accepted. It is an invitation to the other party to make an offer.

It involves the same principle as the later case, *Fisher v Bell* (p. 74) and, like that case, demonstrates the literal way in which the courts interpret the wording of an Act of Parliament.

PHILLIPS v BROOKS LTD
[1919] 2 KB 243

THE FACTS   A man named North went into a jewellers' shop owned by Phillips and selected items of jewellery to a value of £3,000, making out a cheque in payment. When signing the cheque with a false name North said, 'You see who I am, I am Sir George Bullough', and gave an address in St James' Square. Phillips had heard of Sir George Bullough and on checking that the address given by North was the correct one for Sir George Bullough he offered to let North take the jewellery away with him, to which North replied that Phillips had better have the cheque cleared first but as it happened he would like to take a diamond ring away with him as it was for his wife's birthday the next day. Phillips then allowed North to have the ring, valued at £450.

When the cheque for £3,000 was dishonoured North was traced and convicted of obtaining the ring by false pretences but North had immediately pawned the ring for £350 with Brooks Ltd and disposed of the money.

Phillips claimed the return of the ring from Brooks Ltd.

THE DECISION   Phillips, in fact, contracted to sell and deliver the ring to the person who came into his shop, who was not Sir George Bullough but a man in the name of North. Hence North obtained good title to the ring until such time as Phillips sought to avoid the contract of sale for non-payment. So North, having pawned the ring before non-payment was discovered by Phillips, could pass a good title to Brooks Ltd, who were entitled to retain the ring if the pledge was not redeemed.

COMMENTARY   This case illustrates the presumption in the law of contract that in 'face to face' contracts there is an intention to contract with the person *actually present* and not who the person says he or she is.

The presumption can be set aside, but only if a party makes it absolutely clear that the identity of the other party is to be a condition of contracting.

Shopkeepers are not normally interested in the identity of their customers except as a possible indication of ability to pay. So the mistake by Phillips was about an attribute of his customer (the ability to pay).

PHIPPS v ROCHESTER CORPORATION
[1955] 1 QB 450

THE FACTS The plaintiff, a boy aged five, was out blackberrying with his sister, aged seven, and they walked across a building site being developed by the defendants. The defendants had dug a trench on the site 9 feet deep by 2 ½ feet wide. The earth had been heaped to a height of about 4 feet on one side. The plaintiff fell in and broke his leg.

THE DECISION The defendants were not liable because they could not anticipate that a child of this age would not be accompanied by a responsible person and so had not broken their duty of care at common law.

COMMENTARY The Occupiers' Liability Act 1984 now provides that an occupier owes a duty of care to trespassers where:

(a) he is aware of the danger or has reasonable grounds to believe that it exists;

(b) he knows or has reasonable grounds to believe that there are others in the vicinity of the danger, or who may come into the vicinity; and

(c) the risk is such that he may reasonably be expected to offer the other persons some protection.

PINNEL'S CASE
(1602) 5 Co Rep 117a

THE FACTS Pinnel sued Cole because Cole had failed to repay a debt of £8 10s (now £8 50p) on the agreed date, 11 November 1600. Cole's defence was that he had, at Pinnel's request, paid the sum of £5 2s 6d (now £5 12½p) on 1 October 1600 and that Pinnel had accepted this early and lesser payment in settlement of the debt.

THE DECISION It was held that due to a technical fault in the defence by Cole (a failure to plead that the lesser sum was tendered in full settlement) the claim by Pinnel would be upheld.

The common law on the repayment of debt was laid down as follows:

(a) Payment of a lesser sum on the due date cannot be any satisfaction for the whole of the debt. So a creditor who accepts part payment on the due date may still sue for the balance of the debt.

(b) Payment of a lesser sum before the due date at the request of the creditor is good consideration for the creditor's promise to forgo the balance of the debt.

(c) Payment of a lesser sum on the due date either in a different place or accompanied by an object of any value if at the request of the creditor, is good consideration for the creditor's promise to forgo the balance of the debt.

COMMENTARY These common-law rules have remained almost unchanged for nearly 400 years.

If A owes B £100 repayable on 1 January and *if* B is willing to accept say, £10 plus a pencil, the value of the pencil is good consideration to support a promise by B not to claim the balance of £90 still owing by A. It may be rather difficult to find any creditor who will agree to such an arrangement, however good in law.

PITTS v HUNT
[1990] 3 All ER 344

THE FACTS Andrew Pitts, aged 18, and Mark Hunt, aged 16, spent an evening at a disco in Shipton during which time they both consumed a quantity of alcohol. On leaving the disco, Hunt gave a lift to Pitts on his Suzuki trials motor cycle. Hunt held no licence to drive his motor cycle on public roads and was not insured. Pitts knew that Hunt did not have a driving licence or insurance before he accepted a lift as pillion passenger.

Witnesses stated that they saw the motor cycle being driven at speed in a dangerous manner and from one side of the road to the other with the horn being sounded and both driver and passenger shouting 'hooray and yippee'.

The motor cycle collided with an oncoming car, the driver, Hunt, being killed and the pillion passenger, Pitts, being badly injured. Pitts sued the personal representatives of the dead driver, Hunt, in negligence.

At first instance the judge dismissed the claim by Pitts on the gounds that:

(a) Pitts was engaged in a joint illegal enterprise with Hunt (knowing that Hunt did not have either a driving licence or insurance) so that any claim was barred by public policy.

(b) In any event Pitts was 100% contributorily negligent.

Pitts appealed to the Court of Appeal.

THE DECISION The Court of Appeal upheld the first instance decision that the claim was barred by public policy as both parties were engaged in an illegal enterprise. The Court of Appeal also held that it was not possible for Pitts to have been 100% contributorily negligent as the legislation which allows a trial judge to apportion blame (the Law Reform (Contributory Negligence) Act 1945), is based on the premise that there is fault on the part of *both* parties. Where the parties have been engaged in a joint illegal enterprise the correct apportionment of liability is 50% each.

COMMENTARY This case is an important decision on contributory negligence. It seems that the trial judge must divide the blame even if it be 99% to 1%. The case also illustrates the attitude of English law to claims by persons engaged in joint illegal enterprises, namely that the courts will not assist anyone who founds his cause of action on an illegal act. This principle was established in the case of *Holman v Johnson* in 1775 ((1775–1802) All ER Rep 98).

PLANCHÉ v COLBURN
(1831) 8 Bing 14

THE FACTS The plaintiff had agreed to write a book for the defendants, for which he was to be paid £100. He had written part of the book when the defendants abandoned publication.

The plaintiff sued for his fee.

THE DECISION The plaintiff was entitled to half the fee on a *quantum meruit* basis.

COMMENTARY The Latin expression *quantum meruit* means 'as much as he has earned' or 'as much as he deserves'. It is an alternative remedy available in situations where the law is prepared to compel the defendant not to disappoint the plaintiff of the 'fruits of his labour'. Since the plaintiff had laboured to complete half the book, he was entitled to half the fee.

Quantum meruit is available:

(a)   for work done under a contract discharged by the defendant's breach (in *Planché* v *Colburn* the defendant abandoned the publication in which the plaintiff's work was to be published);

(b)   for work done under a contract which subsequenty turns out to be void. (In *Craven Ellis* v *Canons Ltd* the plaintiff was appointed managing director of a company under a contract which was not binding. He did some work for the company and the court awarded him a reasonable remuneration on a *quantum meruit* basis for the work he had done.)

RAFFLES v WICHELHAUS
(1864) 159 ER 375

THE FACTS   Wichelhaus contracted with Raffles for the supply of 125 bales of cotton, the agreed price to be paid on the arrival of the cotton in the UK on a ship, the *Peerless*, from Bombay.

When the cotton arrived in the UK on board a ship *Peerless* which had sailed from Bombay in December, Wichelhaus refused either to accept the cotton or to pay the agreed price.

Raffles sued for a breach of the contract.

In reply Wichelhaus stated that he had agreed to accept and pay for cotton to be shiped from Bombay on a ship *Peerless* sailing from that port in October and had the cotton arrived in the UK as he anticipated, he would have accepted the goods and paid the agreed price.

It transpired that Raffles had no cotton shipped on the *Peerless* sailing from Bombay in October.

THE DECISION   There was nothing in the contract to indicate which ship called *Peerless* was to be the agreed means of transporting the cotton. As there were two ships called *Peerless* sailing from Bombay there was a latent ambiguity in the contract.

If Raffles had in mind the use of the *Peerless* sailing from Bombay in *December* and Wichelhaus had in mind the use of another ship also called *Peerless* sailing from Bombay in *October*, there was no *consensus ad idem* (no real agreement) between the parties and consequently no binding contract.

COMMENTARY   This case illustrates one of the types of operative mistake, that is, a mistake which can render a contract void or voidable. Both parties made different mistakes, known as non-identical mistakes, resulting in them being at cross purposes. This case is a leading example of a bilateral mutual mistake, mutual because both the parties made *different mistakes*.

RAMSGATE VICTORIA HOTEL CO. v MONTEFIORE

(1866) LR 1 Ex 109

THE FACTS   The defendant had offered to buy shares in the plaintiff company in June. The plaintiffs tried to accept this offer in November, by which time the defendant no longer wanted them.

The plaintiffs sued for the purchase price of the shares.

THE DECISION   The six-month delay between the offer in June and the 'acceptance' in November was unreasonable and so the offer had 'lapsed', i.e., it could no longer be accepted and the defendant was not liable for the price of the shares.

COMMENTARY   An offer lapses (i.e., comes to an end/terminates) if it is not accepted within a 'reasonable time'. What is reasonable depends on the circumstances but it is evident that where the contract concerns something that fluctuates in price, e.g., shares, or something which may deteriorate, e.g., fresh food, the time available for acceptance is shorter than for other more durable articles.

Note: an offer comes to an end or terminates on the happening of any of the following events:

   (a)   if not accepted within a reasonable time (as above);
   (b)   if the offeror or offeree dies before acceptance;
((a) and (b) are known as lapse of offer)
   (c)   when revoked/withdrawn before acceptance;
   (d)   when rejected;
   (e)   when a counter-offer is made (see *Hyde* v *Wrench*, p. 93).

R v ADOMAKO
[1994] 2 All ER 79

THE FACTS The defendant was the anaesthetist during an eye operation on a patient. In the course of the operation the tube from the ventilator supplying oxygen to the patient became disconnected. The defendant failed to notice the disconnection for some six minutes before the patient suffered a cardiac arrest, from which he subsequently died. The defendant was charged with manslaughter. He was convicted and appealed to the Court of Appeal on the ground that the judge had wrongly directed the jury by applying the test of gross negligence for manslaughter. The Court of Appeal dismissed the appeal on the ground that the jury had been directed according to the proper test and the evidence justified a verdict of guilty. The defendant appealed to the House of Lords.

THE DECISION The House of Lords confirmed that in order to convict for gross negligence manslaughter the jury must be satisfied that:

(a)   the defedant was in breach of a duty of care towards the victim;
(b)   the breach of duty caused the death of the victim;
(c)   the breach of duty was such as to be characterised as gross negligence and therefore a crime.

They found that on the facts the jury in the defendant's case had been properly directed and therefore the appeal would be dismissed.

COMMENTARY At the trial it was conceded on behalf of the defendant that he had been negligent. The prosecution alleged that he was guilty of *gross* negligence in failing to notice or respond appropriately to obvious signs that a disconnection had occurred and that the patient had ceased to breathe. The question, therefore, was whether the negligence was of such a degree as to justify a conviction for manslaughter, i.e., had (c) above been fulfilled? The jury's judgment at the original trial was that the conduct of the defendant was sufficiently 'gross' to amount to criminal conduct and neither the Court of Appeal nor the House of Lords were minded to alter the judgment.

Note: the defendant was sentenced to six months' imprisonment suspended for 12 months.

THE FACTS Mr Allen was visiting London on business and booked accommodation in a large hotel for 10 days, subsequently extending his stay to 26 days, after which he left the hotel without removing his personal property or paying the hotel bill for £1,286.94. Two days after leaving Mr Allen telephoned the hotel to say that he was in financial difficulties due to delay in some business transactions but that he would collect his personal property and deposit his Australian passport as security for the unpaid hotel bill.

On his return to the hotel Mr Allen was arrested and charged with the offence under section 3(1) of the Theft Act 1978, which provides:

> A person who, knowing that payment on the spot . . . is required or expected from him, dishonestly makes off without having paid as required or expected and with intent to avoid payment of the amount due shall be guilty of an offence.

A jury convicted Mr Allen who appealed to the Court of Appeal. The Appeal Court quashed the conviction on the grounds that the offence was committed only if there was an intention never to pay.

The prosecution appealed to the House of Lords.

THE DECISION The House of Lords affirmed the decision of the Court of Appeal, holding that section 3(1) of the Theft Act 1978 was to be interpreted to mean that the making off offence was to apply only if the person making off had an intention to evade payment altogether.

COMMENTARY This decision reflected the advice of the Criminal Law Revision Committee (13th Report, 1977 Cmnd 6733), that the making off offence should apply only if there was an intention never to pay.

It seems therefore that no criminal liability attaches to a person who takes goods or benefits from services and declines to pay for them on the spot so long as it is made clear that payment will be made at a later date.

This puts the provider of the goods or services into the position of having to extend credit whether he wants to or not.

R v BOWSHER
[1973] RTR 202

THE FACTS On 26 July 1970 Bowsher committed two separate sets of traffic offences.

Bowsher was convicted of the first set of offences on 19 November 1970 and was disqualified from holding a driving licence for six months (until 19 May 1971).

On 2 February 1971 Bowsher was convicted of the second set of offences in a different court and disqualified from holding a driving licence for six months (until 2 August 1971).

On 2 August 1971 the licensing authority returned Bowsher's driving licence to him and he started driving again, believing that his disqualification had expired. Whilst driving on 28 October 1971 Bowsher was stopped and required to produce his licence.

Bowsher was subsequently charged and convicted of driving on 28 October 1971 whilst disqualified, on the basis that 2 × 6 months disqualifications from 19 November 1970 did not expire until 19 November 1971.

Bowsher appealed to the Court of Appeal.

THE DECISION The Court of Appeal held that the conviction for driving on 28 October 1971 whilst disqualified was correct.

The fact that the licensing authority did not correctly apply the provisions of the Road Traffic (Disqualification) Act 1970, by returning the licence on 2 August 1971 instead of on 19 November 1971, provided Bowsher with no defence. Likewise an honest belief by Bowsher that he could resume driving was no defence.

COMMENTARY This case demonstrates that some criminal offences, including most motoring offences, carry strict or absolute liability. In other words, no excuse can be offered for committing the offence. The effect is sometimes to impose criminal liablity on blameless persons, the justification being that the harm that the particular law seeks to prevent could be serious enough to warrant this. If anybody could drive a vehicle, many persons might be harmed.

R v BYRNE

[1960] 3 All ER 1

THE FACTS Byrne strangled a young woman and then sexually mutilated her body. Byrne admitted the crime and was convicted of murder and sentenced to life imprisonment.

Byrne appealed on the grounds that all the medical evidence called at the trial indicated that he was a sexual psychopath, which is an abnormality of the mind which results in uncontrollable, violent, perverted sexual desires, and that he killed as a result of the abnormality of his mind. Consequently Byrne was entitled to rely on the defence of diminished responsibility, so could not be guilty of murder, only manslaughter.

THE DECISION Byrne was entitled to the defence of diminished responsibility, so the conviction for murder would be quashed and a conviction for manslaughter substituted. The sentence of life imprisonment would not be disturbed.

COMMENTARY The defence of diminished responsibility, introduced in the Homicide Act 1957, is intended to deal with situations where the defendant is not normal but not yet insane in the strict legal sense under the 'M'Naghten Rules', which were formulated to decide insanity following the case of Daniel M'Naghten: in 1843 M'Naghten killed Edward Drummond, secretary to Sir Robert Peel, while suffering from insane delusions of being persecuted by Sir Robert Peel.

The defence of diminished responsibility provides that:

A person who kills is not guilty of murder if he/she was suffering from such abnormality of the mind (from any cause) as substantially impaired his/her mental responsibility for the act.

R v CALLENDER
[1992] 3 All ER 51

THE FACTS Callender purported to be a self-employed accountant and represented that he was a member of the Chartered Institute of Management Accountants and held qualifications from the Institute of Marketing. He agreed to prepare accounts and submit income tax and value added tax returns for two small businessmen and collected fees from them on the basis that he had done so. In fact there was no record of any such returns being made.

He was convicted of, among other things, obtaining a pecuniary advantage by deception contrary to section 16(1) of the Theft Act 1968. He appealed against the conviction on the basis that he had offered to provide services as a self-employed fee earning accountant, i.e., an independent contractor and that therefore he had not 'obtained for himself the opportunity to earn remuneration in an *office* or *employment*' as required by the Act under section 16(2)(c).

THE DECISION Although Mr Callender may have been engaged under a contract for services as an independent contractor, he had nevertheless been 'employed' within the terms of the 1968 Act. He was accordingly guilty of obtaining a pecuniary advantage by deception 'in an office or employment' contrary to section 16(2)(c) of the 1968 Act.

COMMENTARY The law distinguishes between a contract 'of service' and a contract 'for services'. A person employed under a contract of service is an employee, whereas a person employed under a contract for services is an independent contractor. Counsel for Mr Callender tried to use this distinction. They contended that the wording of the 1968 Act covered employees, since they were in an 'office or employment' but not independent contractors, since they were self-employed persons and therefore not in an 'office or employment'. This argument was rejected. The Court of Appeal decided that the terms 'office or employment' did extend to cover the engagement of an independent contractor.

THE FACTS Sidney Martins was a French student attending a course in English in London. He was lodging at the house in Lewisham of a Mrs Fox. Also living in the house was Mrs Fox's daughter Jackie, who was engaged to Mr Chan-Fook. Mr Chan-Fook was told by his fiancée that she suspected that Mr Martins had stolen her engagement ring. Mr Chan-Fook and other members of the family strongly questioned Mr Martins about the disappearance of the engagement ring, even though there was no evidence to support the suspicion that he had taken it. Mr Martins, who was not familiar with the English language, was unable to explain the disappearance of the ring. Mr Chan-Fook then dragged Mr Martins upstairs and locked him in a second floor room. Mr Martins tried to escape through the window by making a rope out of knotted sheets attached to the curtain rail. He was injured when the curtain rail broke under his weight and he fell into the garden below.

Mr Chan-Fook was charged with assault occasioning actual bodily harm contrary to section 47 of the Offences Against the Person Act 1861. At his trial the Crown alleged that even if Mr Martins had not suffered any physical injury (the facts concerning the extent of the assault were disputed), he had, nevertheless, been reduced to a mental state which, in itself, amounted to actual bodily harm. The judge directed the jury that an assault which caused an hysterical or nervous condition was capable of being an assault occasioning actual bodily harm. Mr Chan-Fook was convicted and appealed to the Court of Appeal on the grounds of misdirection.

THE DECISION The phrase 'actual bodily harm' in section 47 of the 1861 Act was capable of including psychiatric injury but did not include mere emotions such as fear, distress, panic or an hysterical or nervous condition. Where psychiatric injury was alleged, the Crown should call expert evidence. As there was no evidence to support the allegation that Mr Martins had been caused any psychiatric injury by the assault the appeal was allowed and the conviction quashed.

147

COMMENTARY   The defence case at the trial was that the interrogation and other aspects of the incident had not involved any hitting of Mr Martins, nor had any injuries been caused to him, i.e., the injuries observed by the doctor were attributable solely to his fall. The prosecution chose to introduce into the case an allegation that even if Mr Martins had suffered no physical injury at all as a result of the assault upon him, he had, nevertheless, been reduced to a mental state which, in itself, amounted to actual bodily harm. There was no medical evidence of any psychiatric injury, only evidence that Mr Martins felt abused, humiliated and frightened. The Court of Appeal ruled that these states of mind were not sufficient. The court did, however, accept that, providing that there was expert medical evidence of some identifiable clinical condition, psychiatric injury could be the basis of a charge of assault occasioning actual bodily harm contrary to section 47 of the Offences Against the Person Act 1861.

R v CHURCH
[1965] 2 All ER 72

THE FACTS   Church took a woman into the rear of his van for sexual purposes but was unable to perform the sexual act. After the woman had reproached Church there was a fight in which the woman was knocked out. Church tried for about 30 minutes to revive the woman but was unable to do so. He then dragged the woman out of his van and put her body in a nearby river, where the woman drowned.

   Church was convicted of manslaughter and appealed against the conviction.

THE DECISION   The Court of Appeal held that Church had been properly convicted of gross negligence man-slaughter.

COMMENTARY   A clearer case of gross negligence causing death might be hard to find. The trial judge directed the jury: '. . . if not knowing whether the woman was dead, or not, and not having taken the trouble to find out whether she was dead, or not, he throws her body into the river, you can conclude that this was a negligent act done utterly recklessly . . .'.

R v CLEGG
[1995] 1 All ER 335

THE FACTS Private Lee Clegg, a British soldier stationed in Northern Ireland, was on patrol at night with other members of his unit when another member of the patrol stopped a stolen car at a vehicle checkpoint some distance down the road. The car then accelerated away in the centre of the road with its headlights full on towards Private Clegg and three other members of the patrol. Someone at the checkpoint shouted to stop it and Private Clegg and his three colleagues opened fire at the approaching car. The driver and a rear seat passenger were killed, the latter by a bullet fired from Private Clegg's rifle. He was charged with murder but claimed that he thought the life of a colleague was in danger. The judge, sitting alone, found that the first three shots had been fired in self-defence or defence of a colleague, but that the fourth and fatal shot could not have been, since by this time the car had passed some 50 ft down the road and the soldiers were no longer in any danger. Private Clegg was convicted of murder. His appeal to the Court of Appeal of Northern Ireland was dismissed and he appealed to the House of Lords.

THE DECISION Where a plea of self-defence to a charge of murder failed because the force used was excessive and unreasonable, the homicide could not be reduced to manslaughter. The appeal was dismissed.

COMMENTARY Self-defence in such circumstances is an all or nothing defence: there is no 'halfway house'. As Lord Lloyd observed:

> ... the verdict may be reduced from murder to manslaughter on other grounds, for example, if the prosecution fail to negative provocation where it arises, or fail to prove the requisite intent for murder. But so far as self defence is concerned, it is all or nothing. The defence either succeeds or it fails. If it succeeds the defendant is acquitted. If it fails he is guilty of murder.

Following this case and ones involving 'mercy killings' the inflexibility of the mandatory life sentence has been called into question. Their Lordships emphasised that any change is a matter for Parliament, not the House of Lords in its judicial capacity.

Note: their Lordships also ruled that there is no general defence of acting in obedience to superior orders known to English law, i.e., it is no defence to claim that you are not liable to the sanctions of the law simply because you were ordered by someone in higher authority to do something.

'took off all his clothes except his socks and went back up the ladder'

R v COLLINS

[1972] 2 All ER 1105

THE FACTS Collins was a painter working on a housing estate and he noticed that there was a very attractive young woman living in one of the houses. Collins went to the trouble to find out which was the young woman's bedroom window and one night in July 1971 he put a ladder up to this window, which was wide open, then climbed up the ladder and saw through the window that the young woman was asleep, naked on her bed. Collins then went down the ladder, took off all his clothes except his socks, went back up the ladder and sat perched on the outside of the window sill.

The young woman awoke to see a naked male crouched outside her window in the moonlight and jumped to the conclusion that her boyfriend (with whom she was on very intimate terms) was paying her a nocturnal visit. She sat up and Collins came through the window and joined her on the bed. After they had made love the young woman realised that there was something different about her 'boyfriend', so she turned on the bedside light and discovered her mistake. She slapped Collin's face, who replied, 'Give me a good time tonight', whereupon she went to the bathroom and Collins departed down the ladder.

Collins was convicted of burglary (entering as a trespasser intending to rape). Collins appealed to the Court of Appeal.

THE DECISION The Court of Appeal held that the conviction must be quashed. On the evidence Collins had not entered the bedroom as a trespasser, as the young lady had indicated that he was not unwelcome.

As far as could be ascertained, Collins had remained crouched on the window sill outside the window before the young woman woke up, save for one small part of him which was slightly ahead so entering the bedroom. An entry by a trespasser must be a substantial one and the part of Collins that might have entered before the young woman woke up was not substantial.

COMMENTARY As Edmund Davies LJ said: 'Were the facts put into a novel or portrayed on the stage they could be regarded as so improbable as to be unworthy of serious consideration and as verging at times on farce.'

R v DELLER
(1952) 36 Cr App Rep 184

THE FACTS Deller traded in his Standard motor car for another car, saying that there was no money owing on it and that he was free to sell the car. In fact Deller had previously signed documents which purported to effect the sale of the Standard car to another dealer and at the same time to hire the car back from a finance company. Unknown to Deller this sale and hire back of the Standard car was not effective in law as the documents were defective, so Deller merely *thought* he was falsely pretending that the car was his property when trading it in for another car.

Deller was convicted of falsely pretending to be the owner of the Standard car and he appealed on the grounds that he had, in fact, made no false pretence about the ownership of the car — the previous sale being void meant that Deller was, in truth, the owner of the Standard car at the time of its trade in.

THE DECISION The Court of Appeal held that the conviction must be quashed, as in fact Deller had made no false pretence, having, as one appeal judge put it, 'quite accidentally, and strange as it may sound, dishonestly told the truth'.

COMMENTARY The unusual facts of this case illustrate that all crimes, not merely false pretences, must have a wrongful act (an *actus reus*) and that a 'guilty mind' (a *mens rea*) is not on its own sufficient for a crime to exist.

R v DUDLEY AND STEPHENS
(1884) 14 QBD 273

THE FACTS Four people had been shipwrecked in an open boat a thousand miles from land. They were Captain Dudley, seamen Stephens and Brooks and cabin boy Richard Parker.

After 18 days adrift the Captain convinced Stephens that one of them ought to be sacrificed to save the others, and that the obvious candidate was Richard Parker. He was an orphan, had no wife or family and was already on the brink of death. One day later, Dudley and Stephens killed the cabin boy. Brooks wanted no part in the killing.

All three men survived for three more days by feeding on the boy's body. On the fourth day they were rescued in a very weak condition by a German ship. They were landed at Falmouth in Cornwall. Dudley, Stephens and Brooks went straight to the authorities and explained the reasons for the death of the boy.

THE DECISION The accused were convicted of murder after the jury had returned a special verdict finding that the men would probably have died within the four days had they not fed on the boy's body, that the boy would probably have died before them and that, at the time of the killing, there was no appreciable chance of saving life, except by killing one of the others to eat.

COMMENTARY The defence of 'necessity' was raised and rejected. The case highlights the fact that there is no general defence of necessity — except in cases of self-defence or prevention of violent crimes.

Note: the sentence was commuted to six months' imprisonment.

R v GULLEFER
[1990] 3 All ER 882

THE FACTS Mr Gullefer attended a greyhound race meeting and put a bet of £18 on the dog he fancied to win the last race. After the race had started Gullefer realised that the dog he had backed was not going to win so he jumped on to the track in front of the dogs hoping to distract them and so get the race abandoned. Bets placed with on course bookmakers are returnable if a race is declared 'no race'. Gullefer failed to distract the dogs and was subsequently charged with the attempted theft of £18 from the bookmaker. The Crown Court judge explained to the jury that the Criminal Attempts Act 1981 provides:

> If . . . a person does an act which is more than merely preparatory to the commission of an offence, he is guilty of attempting to commit the offence.

The jury decided that the action of jumping on to the track was more than 'merely preparatory' and accordingly found Gullefer guilty. Gullefer appealed to the Court of Appeal.

THE DECISION In the Court of Appeal the then Lord Chief Justice, Lord Lane, said the question for the court was:

> Might it properly be said that when he (Gullefer) jumped on to the track he was trying to steal £18 from the bookmaker?

Their Lordships held that such an action was not more than merely preparatory and set aside the conviction for attempting to steal £18 from the bookmaker.

COMMENTARY This case illustrates the problem of defining what amounts to a criminal attempt. Before the Criminal Attempts Act 1981, the offence of attempting a crime was a common law offence and it seems doubtful if the intervention of Parliament has resolved the problem.

R v HALLIDAY
[1886–90] All ER Rep 1028

THE FACTS Halliday, who had a reputation for domestic violence, arrived home very drunk and told his wife and daughter to go to bed. Halliday then called out to ask if they had obeyed him and on learning that this was not the case he staggered towards the bedroom shouting threats to his wife.

Mrs Halliday ran to the bedroom window to climb out but was held by her daughter on the window sill, both women being very frightened. Halliday entered the bedroom and said to his daughter, 'Let the bugger go', whereupon the daughter did so and Mrs Halliday fell from the window and broke her leg.

Halliday was convicted of causing his wife grievous bodily harm but appealed.

THE DECISION The Court of Crown Cases Reserved (now the Court of Appeal) held that if a person creates in another person's mind an immediate sense of danger which causes that person to try and escape, then if injury results from the escape attempt, the person who created such a state of mind is liable for the resulting injuries.

The conviction was upheld.

COMMENTARY This case affirms that it is possible to cause serious harm to another without any physical contact, merely by inducing a fear which results in self-inflicted harm.

R v HANCOCK
[1990] 3 All ER 183

THE FACTS With the aid of a metal detector, Mr Hancock found a quantity of silver coins (which were about 2,000 years old) in a field at Wanborough near Guildford. The coins were scattered about the site which is thought to be the site of a Romano-Celtic temple.

Mr Hancock mentioned his find to the local police and was subsequently charged with the theft of treasure trove being the property of the Crown. (Treasure trove is articles of gold or silver which have been hidden by a person unknown with the intention of recovering those articles at some later date.) The trial judge directed the jury that it was sufficient if there was only a possibility that the coins might be treasure trove since the jury had heard conflicting expert evidence that the coins could have been dropped as sacrifices or votive offerings or, alternatively, been deposited as one hoard and scattered by ploughing over the centuries. The jury convicted Mr Hancock of theft of the coins and he appealed to the Court of Appeal.

THE DECISION The Court of Appeal set aside the conviction for theft. It was held that the trial judge had misdirected the jury. A direction that it was sufficient to convict for theft if there was only a possibility that the coins were treasure trove was wrong in law. In order to convict, the jury had to be sure that the coins were 'property belonging to another'.

COMMENTARY This unusual case illustrates the definition of theft contained in the Theft Act 1968, namely: 'A person is guilty of theft if he dishonestly appropriates property belonging to another with the intention of permanently depriving the other of it...' So the property appropriated must be property belonging to another, at the time it is appropriated.

At the time Mr Hancock found the coins, they could have been either treasure trove, and thus Crown property, or they could have been sacrifices or votive offerings abandoned by the respective owners some 2,000 years ago. Consequently, no jury could be sure that at the time of the finds the coins were 'property belonging to another'.

Note: the coins are unique and are now in the British Museum.

R v KINGSTON
[1994] 3 All ER 352

THE FACTS   A man named Penn arranged to blackmail Kingston. In order to do so Penn lured a 15-year-old boy to his flat and gave him a drink laced with drugs. The boy fell asleep on the bed and remembered nothing until he woke next morning. Penn then invited Kingston to his flat and, aware of Kingston's homosexual tendencies, invited him to abuse the boy sexually. Kingston did so. At his trial Kingston claimed that sedative drugs had also been administered to him by Penn and had disinhibited him. This claim was supported by the fact that in pursuance of the attempted blackmail Penn had made a tape recording which contained the remarks by Kingston, 'I don't know why, am I falling asleep?' and 'Have you put something in my coffee?'. Two sedative drugs were found in the flat.

Kingston was convicted of indecent assault and appealed to the Court of Appeal. It allowed his appeal on the basis that there had been a misdirection and the jury should have had the opportunity to consider whether an intent induced by drugs secretly administered was a criminal intent. The prosecution appealed to the House of Lords.

THE DECISION   The appeal was allowed. Although there was no offence if the defendant was so intoxicated that he could not form an intent, a loss of self-control through the acts of a third party did not in general constitute a defence.

COMMENTARY   The House of Lords' decision supported the trial judge's direction to the jury that a drugged intent was still an intent. Their Lordships were satisfied that whatever drug Kingston may have taken had not had such an effect on his mind that he did not intend to do what he did, i.e., he may have lost some self-control but had not lost the ability to form the intent necessary for the offence. A person who intended to do an act which was prohibited by the criminal law could not be exonerated, notwithstanding that the intent arose out of circumstances for which he was not to blame.

R v LLOYD, BHUEE AND ALI
[1985] 2 All ER 661

THE FACTS   Lloyd was the projectionist at an Odeon cinema and Bhuee and Ali were producers of 'pirate' video tapes of feature films and had high speed copying equipment to transfer cine film to master video tape from which 'pirate' copies could be produced. Between showings of feature films in the cinema Lloyd would take the reels of cine film to Bhuee and Ali for copying and all three were caught while making a copy of *The Missionary*.

All three were charged with theft and convicted by a jury.

Appeals were made on the basis that the statutory definition of theft requires an intention to permanently deprive the owner of the property and that the borrowing of the films did not come within the type of borrowing defined by statute as amounting to theft.

THE DECISION   It was held by the Court of Appeal that:

(a)   There was no theft of the cine film.

(b)   The borrowing of the cine films did not constitute theft because the statute required that for a borrowing to amount to theft the 'goodness, virtue or capital value' of the borrowed article must be reduced by that borrowing. The cine films were still able to be shown to paying audiences.

The convictions for theft were quashed; the only offence was a breach of the law of copyright.

COMMENTARY   This case illustrates the problem of deciding just when the borrowing of an article turns into the theft of that article. The relevant law is contained in section 6 of the Theft Act 1968, and has been said to 'sprout obscurity at every phrase'.

It appears that only borrowings that cause direct loss to the owner of the borrowed article can constitute theft. For example, a borrowed season ticket which is returned to the owner the day before it expires would cause loss to the owner, and so would amount to the theft of that season ticket.

R v MILLER
[1983] 1 All ER 978

THE FACTS Miller was sleeping in an unoccupied furnished house without the consent of the owner. One night Miller fell asleep while smoking and woke up to find that the bedding was on fire. Miller then went into another bedroom and went back to sleep, only to be awakened again by the fire brigade. When asked what had happened, Miller replied, 'I hadn't got anything to put the fire out with, so I just left it'.

Miller was charged with arson (causing damage by fire) under the Criminal Damage Act 1971, which provides:

> A person who without lawful excuse destroys or damages any property belonging to another intending to destroy or damage any such property or being reckless as to whether any such property would be destroyed or damaged shall be guilty of an offence . . .

Miller was convicted by a jury and on appeal the Court of Appeal upheld the conviction. Miller further appealed to the House of Lords.

THE DECISION It was held by the House of Lords that a person who, on becoming aware of a danger he has created, either:

(a)   consciously takes the risk of further harm; *or*
(b)   gives no thought to there being any such risk if it is an obvious risk;

is reckless.
The conviction was upheld.

COMMENTARY This case involves the very difficult issue of 'recklessness' and illustrates that a *failure* to act, as opposed to a physical act (an *actus reus*) can, in some circumstances, attract criminal liability. In the House of Lords Lord Diplock expressed dislike of the term *actus reus*, as it suggests that there must be some positive act to attract criminal liability, whereas it is the conduct of the accused person that matters.

163

R v MORRIS
[1983] 3 WLR 697

THE FACTS Morris took goods from the shelves of a supermarket and replaced the price labels attached to the goods with other labels showing a lesser price. At the checkout Morris was asked for, and paid, the lesser price. After leaving the supermarket Morris was arrested and charged with theft, having 'dishonestly appropriated property belonging to another'.

A jury convicted Morris and he appealed to the Court of Appeal which upheld the conviction. Morris further appealed to the House of Lords.

THE DECISION It was held by the House of Lords that the statutory definition of 'appropriates' contained in section 3(1) of the Theft Act 1968, namely:

> any assumption by a person of the rights of an owner amounts to an appropriation

was to be interpreted to mean any assumption by a person of *any* of the rights of an owner. It was not necessary to assume *all* the rights of an owner.

The House of Lords also held that the concept of appropriation involved only acts amounting to either adverse interference with or usurpation of the rights of the owner. Price label switching could interfere with one of the rights of the owner, namely to decide the selling price.

The conviction was upheld.

COMMENTARY This decision partly clarifies the law applicable to price label switching in supermarkets, etc. But as Lord Roskill put it: '... if a shopper with some perverted sense of humour, intending only to create confusion and nothing more, ... switches labels, I do not think that the act of label switching alone is without more an appropriation'.

R v NEDRICK
[1986] 3 All ER 1

THE FACTS Nedrick, who bore a grudge against a woman, poured paraffin through the letter-box of the woman's house and set it alight. A child died in the resulting fire and Nedrick was charged with murder. Nedrick admitted starting the fire intending merely to frighten the woman, not to kill anyone, since when he was asked why he started the fire he replied, 'Just to wake her up and frighten her'.

By a majority the jury convicted Nedrick of murder, and he was sentenced to life imprisonment. Nedrick appealed to the Court of Appeal.

THE DECISION It was held by the Court of Appeal that a person could not be guilty of murder unless either:

(a) he intended to kill or cause serious harm; *or*
(b) he appreciated that death or serious harm was an almost certain consequence of his action.

The conviction for murder was quashed and a conviction for manslaughter was substituted with a sentence of 15 years' imprisonment.

COMMENTARY This decision develops further the law regarding criminal liability for acts resulting in death which may be described as reckless acts rather than intentional acts. With reckless acts the wrongdoer may, or may not, have thought about the possible consequences of that act.

A jury in this sort of case must now be directed that they cannot find the necessary *mens rea* (guilty mind) for murder unless they are sure that the defendant appreciated that either death or serious harm from his act was a 'virtual certainty'.

R v QUICK
[1973] 3 All ER 347

THE FACTS Quick was a male nurse in a mental hospital and suffered from diabetes, for which he took prescribed amounts of the drug insulin. Quick attacked and injured a patient and was charged with an assault causing actual bodily harm.

Quick claimed that the assault took place whilst he was suffering from hypoglycaemia (a lack of sugar), a condition common to users of insulin, and that as a result of his condition he did not know what he was doing. Consequently he was entitled to the defence of 'automatism' (involuntary actions resulting from a failure of the normal link between a person's mind and his actions).

At the trial the judge ruled that Quick could only put up the defence of insanity, so Quick changed his plea to 'guilty' and then appealed against the ruling by the trial judge.

THE DECISION It was held by the Court of Appeal that the trial judge was in error to hold that Quick could only rely on the defence of insanity. Quick was entitled to have his defence of 'automatism' left to the jury to decide.

As it was therefore not certain that the jury would have convicted Quick, the conviction was quashed as unsatisfactory.

COMMENTARY The Court of Appeal had to consider if the defendant's condition at the time of the assault amounted to 'a defect of reason from disease of the mind', which is the essential requirement for establishing insanity. Clearly the defendant's mental condition was due to an external condition, namely, the taking of insulin followed by a lack of sugar, and not to a bodily disorder in the nature of a disease which disturbed the working of his mind.

It may be thought strange that a nurse would not recognise the onset of hypoglycaemia and immediately correct it by eating a lump of sugar.

R v R
[1991] 4 All ER 481

THE FACTS The case concerns an appeal by a husband sentenced for attempted rape of his wife. The couple were married in August 1984 and they had one son born in 1985. On 11 November 1987 the couple separated for about two weeks but resumed cohabitation at the end of that period. On 21 October 1989 the wife left the matrimonial home with the son and went to live with her parents, leaving a letter informing her husband that she intended to petition for divorce.

Neither party had instituted divorce proceedings. On 12 November 1989 the husband forced his way into the house of his wife's parents, who were out at the time, and attempted to have sexual intercourse with his wife against her will. He was charged with rape and assault occasioning actual bodily harm. The defence submitted that a husband could not in law be guilty as a principal of the offence of raping his own wife. The judge ruled that a wife's consent to sexual intercourse could be terminated and had been terminated in this case. The husband then pleaded guilty of attempted rape and to assault occasioning actual bodily harm. His appeal to the Court of Appeal was dismissed but leave to appeal to the House of Lords was granted.

THE DECISION The rule that a husband cannot be criminally liable for raping his wife if he has sexual intercourse with her without her consent no longer forms part of the law of England since a husband and wife are now to be regarded as equal partners in marriage. The decision of the Court of Appeal was affirmed.

COMMENTARY The case is a good illustration of the process by which an appeal reaches the House of Lords. The husband had been sentenced at Leicester Crown Court to three years' imprisonment for attempted rape and to 18 months' imprisonment for assault occasioning actual bodily harm. He appealed to the Court of Appeal Criminal Division on the ground that the judge 'made a wrong decision in law in ruling that a man may rape his wife when the consent to intercourse which his wife gives in entering the contract of marriage has been revoked neither by order of a court nor by agreement between the parties'.

The Court of Appeal delivered a 'reserved' judgment dismissing the appeal but certifying the following point of law of general public importance as being involved in its decision, namely, 'Is a husband criminally liable for raping his wife?'. Rape is defined by section 1(1) of the Sexual Offences (Amendment) Act 1976 as having unlawful intercourse with a woman without her consent. In coming to their landmark decision the House of Lords overturned the long established common law principle that intercourse between man and wife was lawful, notwithstanding that it was obtained by force.

R v SECRETARY OF STATE FOR EMPLOYMENT EX PARTE EQUAL OPPORTUNITIES COMMISSION

The Times, 4 March 1994

THE FACTS The Employment Protection (Consolidation) Act 1978 restricts the rights of part-time employees to compensation for unfair dismissal and to redundancy pay to those who have either worked for more than 16 hours per week or who have worked for at least eight hours a week for at least five years.

The restriction was highlighted by the case of Mrs Patricia Day who was made redundant after working as a cleaner for Hertfordshire County Council for 11 hours a week for just under five years. The Equal Opportunities Commission sought a Declaration by way of Judicial Review that the provisions of the 1978 Act conflicted with European law by being a form of indirect discrimination against female workers contrary to Article 119 of the Treaty of Rome. The basis of the indirect discrimination claim was that the majority of workers who worked for more than 16 hours a week were male but the majority of workers who worked for less than 16 hours a week were female.

The Divisional court refused the application for a Declaration and, on appeal, this refusal was upheld by a majority of the Court of Appeal. The Commission further appealed to the House of Lords.

THE DECISION By a 4:1 majority the House of Lords rejected the claim by the Secretary of State that the restrictions in the 1978 Act would promote the availability of part-time employment by reducing the cost to employers of employing part-time staff and that the discrimination was therefore justified and in compliance with European law.

Their Lordships held that no evidence had been produced to support the claim that the restrictions in the 1978 Act resulted in the greater availability of part-time employment. A Declaration was granted that the restrictions in the 1978 Act on the entitlement of part-time employees to compensation for unfair dismissal and for redundancy pay were contrary to Article 119 of the Treaty of Rome and to the subsequent Directives of the Council of Ministers.

R v SECRETARY OF STATE FOR EMPLOYMENT
EX PARTE EQUAL OPPORTUNITIES
COMMISSION — *continued*

COMMENTARY This case is another outstanding example of the supremacy of European law over domestic law and puts part-time workers on an equal basis with full-time workers for claims of unfair dismissal compensation and for redundancy pay.

R v SECRETARY OF STATE FOR HEALTH
EX PARTE US TOBACCO INTERNATIONAL INC
[1992] 1 All ER 212

THE FACTS US Tobacco set up a factory in Scotland to produce snuff products for oral use. By 1985 US Tobacco were the sole producers in the United Kingdom, the products being sold under the brand name 'Skoal Bandits'. In 1986 the government advisory committee on use of chemicals in food and other products proposed a ban on oral snuff because of evidence of a causal link with certain forms of cancer.

In 1988 the Secretary of State announced that he intended to use the powers conferred by the Consumer Protection Act 1987 to make regulations banning oral snuff. The Oral Snuff (Safety) Regulations were laid before Parliament in December 1989. US Tobacco sought an order of *certiorari* to quash the Regulations by way of Judicial Review on the grounds, *inter alia*, that the Secretary of State had failed to comply with the provisions of the Consumer Protection Act 1987 which require:

> Where the Secretary of State proposes to make safety regulations it shall be his duty before he makes them to consult such organisations as appear to him to be representative of interests substantially affected by the proposal.

The Minister had flatly refused US Tobacco access to the evidence and to the reasoning of the advisory committee.

THE DECISION The order of *certiorari* would issue. In the words of Taylor LJ (now LCJ):

> . . . I can see no ground in logic or reason for declining to show the applicants the text of the advice. To conceal from them the scientific advice which directly led to the ban, was in my judgment unfair and unlawful.

COMMENTARY This case shows that claims to secrecy by government departments, at least in matters of consumer safety, are not upheld by the judiciary

171

R v SECRETARY OF STATE FOR HEALTH EX PARTE US TOBACCO INTERNATIONAL INC
— continued

where a clear duty can be shown to exist to disclose all relevant information to interested parties and that delegated legislation will be struck down in appropriate circumstances.

After consultations, new regulations were issued, the Tobacco for Oral Use (Safety) Regulations 1992.

R v SECRETARY OF STATE FOR TRANSPORT EX PARTE FACTORTAME LTD
C–213/89, [1990] 3 WLR 852, ECJ

THE FACTS   Factortame, a Spanish company, were the owners and operators of 95 fishing boats which were registered as 'British' under the Merchant Shipping Act 1894. This allowed the boats to fish against the fishing quota allocated to the UK by the European Union, a practice known as 'quota hopping'. Following an outcry from UK fishermen, Parliament, in the Merchant Shipping Act 1988 and subsequent regulations, changed the registration requirements for fishing boats so that boats previously registered as 'British' would have to re-register and could only do so if not less than 75% of the owners/shareholders were British citizens resident and domiciled in the UK. The new regulations would mean that the Factortame boats could not re-register as 'British' and consequently would not be able to fish against the UK fishing quota after April 1989.

Factortame applied for a Declaration by Judicial Review that the Merchant Shipping Act 1988 conflicted with European law. The Divisional Court referred to the European Court and purported to *suspend the 1988 Act* as it applied to Factortame. The Court of Appeal and the House of Lords reversed the decision to suspend the 1988 Act, but the Lords ruled that it should not be enforced pending the decision of the European Court.

THE DECISION   The European Court held that the requirement that owners/shareholders be at least 75% British citizens was contrary to Article 52 of the Treaty of Rome (discrimination against nationals of member states on grounds of nationality).

COMMENTARY   This case highlights the relationship between UK law and European law and clearly establishes the supremacy of European law. The interim decision of the European Court, that when a national court was dealing with a case involving European law it was permissible under Community law for that national court to set aside domestic law, has caused much concern. The prospect of any English court 'setting aside' an Act of Parliament has been described by one judge (Sir Thomas Bingham MR) as a 'constitutional enormity'.

R v THORNTON

The Times, 29 July 1991

THE FACTS Mrs Thornton married in 1988 but the marriage was not successful owing to the drinking habits of her husband and Mrs Thornton suffered abuse and violence on a number of occasions. One evening in June 1989 Mrs Thornton asked her husband, who had been asleep on a couch, to come up to bed but he declined and made insulting remarks. Mrs Thornton then went to the kitchen, found a carving knife, sharpened it and returend to the living room. After further exchanges with her husband, Mrs Thornton plunged the knife into her husband, killing him. When the police arrived Mrs Thornton said '... I sharpened the knife so I could kill him ...'. Mrs Thornton was charged with murder and convicted, the jury rejecting the defence of provocation (which would have reduced murder to manslaughter). Mrs Thornton appealed on the grounds that provocation shoud not be limited to acts done in the moment of a temporary loss of self-control (the 'heat of the moment').

THE DECISION The Court of Appeal upheld the conviction for murder. The court held that provocation only applied to acts done in the moment of a temporary loss of self-control and any acts done after a 'cooling-off' period were not covered by the provocation defence.

COMMENTARY It is clear that in law a person who is provoked cannot take time to think about or prepare any retaliatory actions and then claim the defence of provocation.

Students might care to consider how long is 'the moment of a temporary loss of self-control'.

R v TOLSON
(1889) 23 QBD 168

THE FACTS The defendant was deserted by her husband in 1881 and heard from reliable sources that he had been drowned while on a voyage to America. More than five years later, believing herself to be a widow, she married again. Her husband reappeared in 1887 and she was charged with bigamy.

THE DECISION She was not guilty. It was a defence to the charge to show that she had an honest and reasonable belief that her husband was dead.

COMMENTARY Mistake is a defence where it prevents the defendant from having the necessary intent (*mens rea*) which the law requires for the crime with which he is charged.

Bigamy is the crime committed by a person who, being lawfully married, goes through a form of marriage with another person during the life of the first husband or wife. The second 'marriage' is void.

Mrs Tolson's defence of mistake to the charge of bigamy was allowed because she believed in good faith and on reasonable grounds that her husband was dead — her husband had been reported drowned at sea and had been missing for more than five years. She could therefore claim that, had she known the true facts, the crime of bigamy would not have been committed.

Note: (i) An unreasonable belief would not afford a defence. If Mrs Tolson had heard a rumour in 1885 that her husband was still alive, she probably could not have pleaded mistake. (ii) Mistake of law is no excuse — *ignorantia legis haud excusat*. This reflects the premise that everyone is presumed to know the law.

R v TOLSON

'Her husband reappeared . . .'

REID v RUSH & TOMPKINS GROUP plc
[1989] 3 All ER 228

THE FACTS Mr Reid took employment with Rush & Tompkins on a road project in Ethiopia which involved driving his employer's Land Rover. In January 1984, whilst driving the vehicle on a bush road, during the course of his employment, Mr Reid was badly injured in a collision with an oncoming lorry which did not stop and thus the identity of the driver etc. could not be discovered. Ethiopia has no requirement for compulsory third party insurance or any system of compensating the victims of uninsured drivers.

Mr Reid was so badly injured that he could do no work for over three years after the accident, and sued his employer for compensation on the basis that the employer had failed in an alleged duty of care to insure their employee whilst employed in Ethiopia or, alternatively, had failed to advise their employee to obtain his own insurance. At first instance the claim was struck out as showing no reasonable cause of action. Mr Reid appealed to the Court of Appeal.

THE DECISION The Court of Appeal upheld the striking out of the claim. An employer who engaged staff for overseas projects had no duty of care to insure such employees or to advise the employees to obtain their own insurance unless the contract of employment contained either an express or an implied term to that effect. The court declined to extend the general common law duties of an employer to include a duty to protect an employee from economic loss. The fact that Rush & Tompkins might be aware of the special risks of working in Ethiopia did not import any term into the contract of employment that entitled the plaintiff to recover for the loss he had sustained.

COMMENTARY This decision was followed in the case of *Cook* v *Square D Ltd* (see p. 52). Whilst employers have been required since 1972 to have insurance against claims by employees for injury/disease arising out of employment, this requirement (Employers' Liability (Compulsory Insurance) Act 1969), applies *only* to employment in the United Kingdom or employment on offshore installations (oil rigs). Employees who take overseas appointments are therefore not protected by English law and should take suitable precautions to protect themselves.

ROBERTS v GRAY
[1913] 1 KB 520

THE FACTS The defendant, a minor, agreed to accompany the plaintiff, a professional billiard player, on a world tour, during which he would receive instruction. A dispute arose and the minor refused to go.

THE DECISION The contract was valid and binding on the minor as it was a 'beneficial contract of service'. He was therefore liable and damages were awarded to the plaintiff for breach of contract.

COMMENTARY Contracts made by minors are valid and binding if they fall into either of two categories;

(a) contracts for 'necessaries' (see *Nash v Inman*, p. 120);
(b) beneficial contracts of service.

This case falls within (b), which covers any situation where a minor enters into a contract involving education, training, apprenticeship, etc. provided that, taken as a whole, it is for his benefit (see *De Francesco v Barnum*, p. 60).

Note: in determining what constitutes a beneficial contract of service the courts are prepared to include relationships which bear the 'hallmarks' of apprenticeship, etc. In the case *Doyle v White City Stadium*, for instance, a contract was made between a professional boxer (a minor) and the British Boxing Board of Control, under which the minor received a licence to box and agreed to comply with the rules of the Board. These included a term that if he were disqualified the money he was to receive for the fight would be withheld. The boxer fought a contest and was disqualified. He sued for the money and was unsuccessful, since he was bound by the agreement and its terms:

(a) It was analagous to a contract of service (i.e., it resembled an apprenticeship).
(b) It was beneficial (i.e., it enabled him to learn his 'trade' and the terms of the licence protected both contestants).

ROBERTSON v RIDLEY AND ANOTHER
[1989] 2 All ER 474

THE FACTS Mr Robertson was a member of the Sale & Ashton Conservative Club, and on 20 April 1985 he was riding his motor cycle out of the Club grounds when he failed to see a pothole in the drive and was thrown off his motor cycle. As a result of the accident, Mr Robertson sustained injuries for which he claimed £3,500 in compensation from the chairman and secretary of the Conservative Club. The basis of the claim was that the rules of the Club made the chairman and secretary responsible, in law, for the conduct of the Club which placed upon those officials the duty to ensure that the Club premises were kept in a reasonable state of safety and repair.

At first instance it was held that:

(a) In the absence of an express provision in the rules of the Club that the officers were to be responsible for the condition of the Club premises, there was no duty of care upon those officers of the Club towards the members to ensure that the premises were safe.

(b) The general common law rule applied that there was no liability between a club and its members on the one hand and an individual member on the other hand.

The claim was dismissed. Mr Robertson appealed to the Court of Appeal.

THE DECISION The Court of Appeal held that at common law, the officers and members of the committee of a club which is an unincorporated association, as in this case, have no duty of care towards the members of the club. The expression that the chairman and secretary be 'responsible in law' means that those officers shall be responsible for only the duties cast upon the club by law before the rules come into existence. The first instance decision to dismiss the claim was upheld.

COMMENTARY This case raises a problem, namely, who is the 'occupier' of such a club for the purposes of the Occupiers' Liability Act 1957? This statute casts upon the 'occupier' of premises a duty to take

ROBERTSON v RIDLEY AND ANOTHER —
continued

reasonable care to ensure that all visitors to the premises will be safe. (See *O'Connor* v *Swan & Edgar and Carmichael*, p. 126).

ROBINSON v KILVERT

(1889) 41 Ch D 88

THE FACTS The defendant began to manufacture paper boxes in the cellar of a house. The floor above was leased to the plaintiff. The defendant used a boiler which created hot, dry air. This raised the temperature on the floor above, damaging brown paper which the plaintiff warehoused there.

The plaintiff sued in the tort of nuisance.

THE DECISION The defendant was not liable in nuisance.

The paper stored by the plaintiff was exceptionally sensitive to heat. Ordinary paper would not have been damaged by the heating process, which did not inconvenience the plaintiff's workmen.

COMMENTARY This case illustrates that an action in nuisance will not be successful if the loss arose as a result of the particular sensitivity of the plaintiff or his property, i.e., there is no redress for damage due solely to the exceptionally delicate nature of the operations carried on by an injured party.

Lord Justice Lopes commented, 'A man who carries on an exceptionally delicate trade cannot complain because it is injured by his neighbour doing something lawful on his property, if it is something which would not injure anything but an exceptionally delicate trade'.

Note: nuisance is an interference with a person's use or enjoyment of land. A plaintiff in nuisance need not own the land; occupation is sufficient. In this case a tenant sued.

SAYERS v HARLOW URBAN DISTRICT COUNCIL
[1958] 2 All ER 342

THE FACTS The plaintiff sustained injuries after she was trapped because of a faulty lock in a toilet maintained by the defendants. She fell while attempting to climb out by standing on the toilet-roll holder.

She sued for damages in the tort of negligence.

THE DECISION The defendants were principally to blame but the plaintiff was also at fault for standing on a 'revolving object'. Her 'contributory negligence' was assessed at 25% and her damages were accordingly reduced by that amount.

COMMENTARY The Law Reform (Contributory Negligence) Act 1945 provides that where both parties are partly to blame for a loss, a claimant's damages will be reduced in proportion to the extent to which they were responsible for that loss.

Mrs Sayers was considered to be 25% to blame, so the damages she received were 25% less than she would have received had the defendants been entirely to blame.

A common application of this principle arises in the case of car accidents — a passenger injured due to the negligent driving of another will have his damages reduced if he was not wearing a seat belt, as is regarded as being contributorily negligent for his own injuries.

Note: where the plaintiff has been put at risk by the defendant's negligence, compelling him to choose between two or more risky alternatives, he is not guilty of contributory negligence if his choice turns out to be a mistaken one, e.g., jumping from a bus in the mistaken but reasonable belief that it was about to overturn.

'She fell while attempting to climb out by standing on the toilet-roll holder'

SIMPKINS v PAYS
[1955] 3 All ER 10

THE FACTS A grandmother, granddaughter and lodger entered a newspaper fashion competition. They won a prize of £750 but the grandmother (the defendant) refused to pay and the lodger sued for his share.

THE DECISION Although this appeared to be in the nature of a domestic agreement, there was evidence of an intention to create legal relations — it was a joint enterprise and they had agreed to 'go shares'.

The plaintiff was legally entitled to his share, i.e., £250.

COMMENTARY A contract is an agreement that is intended to have legal consequences.

The general rule is that agreements of a domestic/social type are not intended to be legally binding. In the words of Atkin LJ,

> It is necessary to remember that there are agreements between parties which do not result in contracts within the meaning of that term in our law. The ordinary example is where two parties agree to take a walk together or where there is an offer and an acceptance of hospitality. Nobody would suggest in ordinary circumstances that those agreements result in what we know as a contract, ... even though there may be what as between other parties would constitute consideration .... They are not contracts because the parties did not intend that they should be attended by legal consequences.

This does not mean that agreements of a domestic/social nature are *never* legally binding; the 'presumption' that they are not legally binding can be 'rebutted' — as illustrated by this case. The parties were in a domestic/social relationship but the court detected an intention to create legal relations from the informal syndicate they had created.

SMITH v STAGES & DARLINGTON INSULATION CO. LTD

[1989] 1 All ER 833

Note: the original plaintiff, a Mr Machin, died before the case was heard so Ms Smith, his administratrix, continued the action on behalf of the estate of Mr Machin.

THE FACTS Messrs Machin and Stages were employed by Darlington Insulation as insulation installers in various power stations so that they had no one permanent place of work. In August 1977, both employees were working at the Drakelow power station in Burton-on-Trent and were instructed to go to the Pembroke power station in South Wales to carry out an urgent insulation job. This work was to start on Tuesday, 23 August, and be completed by 8.30 am on Monday, 29 August. The employer set aside two working days for travel, Monday, 22 August, and Tuesday, 30 August (Monday, 29 August, was a paid Bank Holiday), on both days the employees would be paid a full eight hours and additionally paid their travel expenses based on the rail fare. However, the employer allowed its employees to travel whenever they preferred to do so and by whatever means they chose.

Messrs Machin and Stages managed to complete the work only by working all day and all night on the Sunday, 28 August but decided to travel home in Mr Stages' car on the Monday, 29 August and take the Tuesday as their Bank Holiday day. On the way home to Burton-on-Trent the car left the road, went through a wall injuring both the driver, Mr Stages, and the passenger, Mr Machin. The accident was due to negligent driving by Mr Stages and Mr Machin claimed compensation, joining the employer as co-defendant, on the basis that as the employees were in the course of their employment the employer had vicarious liability for the negligence of Mr Stages.

At first instance it was held that the employees were not in the course of their employment at the time of the accident so that the employer was not vicariously liable to the estate of Mr Machin. The plaintiff appealed to the Court of Appeal, who reversed the first instance decision, holding that the employer was vicariously liable to the estate of Mr Machin. The employer obtained leave to appeal to the House of Lords against the Appeal Court ruling on their vicarious liability.

THE DECISION The House of Lords affirmed the decision of the Court of Appeal that the employer was vicariously liable to the estate of Mr Machin as both employees were in the course of their employment at the time of the accident, hence the employer was liable for the negligence of its employee, Mr Stages.

COMMENTARY The meaning of 'in the course of the employment' in cases involving vicarious liability is the subject of some doubt. Lord Goff stressed the difference in travel between different places of work and travel between home and a fixed place of work. His Lordship considered that the fact that travelling time is paid is important but not decisive.

SPRING v GUARDIAN ASSURANCE AND OTHERS
The Times, 8 July 1994

THE FACTS Mr Spring was employed as office manager and sales director designate by Corinium Mortgage Services Ltd, who were agents for the sale of Guardian Assurance insurance policies. In 1989 Guardian Assurance bought Corinium and the chief executive of Guardian, a Mr Siderfin, did not get on well with Mr Spring. About three weeks after the take over Mr Spring was dismissed without any explanation.

Mr Spring sought employment with the Scottish Amicable Life Assurance Society who obtained a reference on Mr Spring from his former employer, Guardian Assurance. As a result of the reference Scottish Amicable declined to employ Mr Spring. Mr Spring claimed damages for malicious falsehood and negligence in respect of the Guardian reference. At first instance the judge described the reference as 'so strikingly bad as to amount to ... the kiss of death to his (Mr Spring's) career in insurance' and held that whilst the claim of malicious falsehood could not be upheld Guardian had failed to exercise reasonable care in the preparation of the reference and were thus liable in negligence.

Guardian Assurance appealed to the Court of Appeal against the finding of liability in negligence for the reference and the Appeal Court reversed the first instance decision, holding that there was no liability in negligence for the reference. Mr Spring further appealed to the House of Lords.

THE DECISION By a 4:1 majority their Lordships reversed the decision of the Court of Appeal holding that, under the principles laid down in *Hedley Byrne* v *Heller*, where the relationship between the parties was that of employer and employee a duty of care was owed by the employer to the employee in respect of the preparation of any reference. The duty of care arose because the employer was possessed of special knowledge derived from his experience of the employee's character, skill and diligence whilst working for that employer.

SPRING v GUARDIAN ASSURANCE AND
OTHERS — *continued*

COMMENTARY This decision indicates a further extension of the law of negligence, although it should be noted that the dissenting Law Lord (Lord Keith) held that such a extension was not justified as only pure economic loss was involved.

For the case of *Hedley Byrne & Co. Ltd* v *Heller & Partners Ltd* [1963] 2 All ER 575, see p. 86.

STILK v MYRICK
(1809) 170 ER 1168

THE FACTS   Stilk, a merchant seaman, signed up for a voyage from London to the Baltic ports and return. The ship's articles (the crew agreement) provided that Stilk was to be paid at the rate of £5 per month and the articles contained a term that all the members of the crew would do all they could to ensure the safe return of the ship 'under all the emergencies of the voyage'.

In the course of the voyage two crew members left the ship and the captain was unable to obtain replacement crew at the Baltic ports. The captain thereupon agreed with Stilk and the other remaining crew members that if they sailed the ship back to London short-handed, the wages of the two crew members who had left the ship would be shared out amongst them.

The owners of the ship refused to honour the agreement made by the captain, so Stilk sued for his share of the wages of the deserted crew.

THE DECISION   The agreement made by the captain of the ship with Stilk and the other crew members was not binding, as Stilk and the others had not given any consideration to support the agreement.

The desertion of the two crew members at one of the Baltic ports was an 'emergency of the voyage' and under the terms of the original agreement (the articles) Stilk was under an obligation to do all in his power to ensure the safe return of the ship.

COMMENTARY   This seemingly unfair decision has to be looked at in the circumstances prevailing at the time when seamen accepted very onerous conditions, including that if freight was lost on a voyage they would not get paid.

This case illustrates the principle in the law of contract that a promise cannot be enforced unless there is good consideration given in return for that promise and, legally, Stilk did nothing for the promise of extra pay, since he did no more than he had originally promised to do.

Note: this decision was approved by the Court of Appeal in *Williams* v *Roffey Bros & Nicholls Ltd* (p. 207–8).

STOREY v ASHTON
(1869) LR 4 QB 476

THE FACTS The defendant employed a driver, who was on an errand when he took a detour to do a favour for a fellow employee. He negligently knocked down and injured the plaintiff who sued on the basis that the defendant was vicariously liable for the negligence of his employee.

THE DECISION The defendant was not liable as, at the time of the accident, his employee was acting outside the course of his employment.

COMMENTARY The expression 'vicarious liability' refers to the situation where one person is liable for the wrongdoing of another. It can arise in a number of situations, e.g., parent and child, but it occurs most commonly in the employer/employee and the employer/independent contractor relationships.

The justification for imposing liability on an employer is that it:

(a)   stops him hiring an employee to commit a tort;
(b)   encourages him to maintain a safe system of work;
(c)   is generally the case that he is in a better financial position to compensate the injured party.

This case illustrates that an employer is not vicariously liable for the torts of an employee committed outside 'the course of his employment' or who is on 'a frolic of his own'. Had the detour been slight or unavoidable, the employer would have been liable.

Note: the employer *and* employee are liable and may be sued 'jointly and severally'. This means they are individually liable and collectively liable, so the plaintiff can either sue one or the other or both. Usually only the employer is sued, on the basis that he is more likely to be able to pay the damages. If the employer is sued he may recover some or all of the loss from the employee.

SUTCLIFFE v PRESSDRAM LTD
[1990] 1 All ER 269

THE FACTS In January 1981, Peter Sutcliffe was arrested and charged with the murder of 13 women and the attempted murder of seven women. The case attracted intense interest from newspaper reporters who tried to get stories from Mrs Sonia Sutcliffe and other members of the family.

The magazine 'Private Eye', published by Pressdram Ltd, printed an article which claimed that whilst her husband was awaiting trial Mrs Sutcliffe had 'done a deal' with a national newspaper to sell her story for £250,000. Later 'Private Eye' repeated this story and claimed that Mrs Sutcliffe had lied to the police to protect her husband and made false claims for social security.

In 1987 (just within the six-year limitation period), Mrs Sutcliffe started an action for damages for libel against the publishers on the basis that the articles in 'Private Eye' meant that, finding herself married to a murderer, she sought to sell her story for £250,000. The publishers contended that the articles only meant that Mrs Sutcliffe was prepared to consider obtaining a financial benefit on her notoriety as the wife of a multiple killer, which was a justifiable comment.

At first instance the jury, after hearing the evidence presented, decided that the articles were libellous and assessed damages at £600,000. Pressdram Ltd indicated that they would appeal, that the damages awarded were excessive and the judge released only £25,000 of the damages award.

THE DECISION The Court of Appeal held that the award of £600,000 was excessive and was therefore set aside. The Court of Appeal was prepared to order a new trial on the amount of damages but both parties indicated they would like the court to decide the amount of damages. Before this could be done the parties agreed an amount of £60,000, plus Mrs Sutcliffe's costs of £33,677.58.

COMMENTARY It should be borne in mind that at present, legal aid is not available for defamation actions, the costs of which are very considerable. If the

SUTCLIFFE v PRESSDRAM LTD — *continued*

plaintiff loses the claim, they are liable not only for their own costs but also for the legal costs of the other party. In this case the amount Mrs Sutcliffe risked liability for was probably over £70,000, as Pressdram Ltd employed a Queen's Counsel for their defence.

The financial risks involved in defamation cases deter many people who may have suffered some damage to their reputation, and proposals have been made that minor defamation cases should be dealt with by a special tribunal rather than in the High Court.

SWEET v PARSLEY
[1969] 1 All ER 347

THE FACTS Miss Sweet owned a farmhouse near Oxford but did not reside there, letting all the rooms except one to students. Miss Sweet used the room she retained during her occasional visits to collect the rents and check over her property.

The police found some of the students smoking cannabis in the farmhouse and Miss Sweet was convicted by the magistrates' court of an offence under section 5(b) of the Dangerous Drugs Act 1965, which provided:

> [If a person] is concerned in the management of any premises used for any such purpose as aforesaid, he shall be guilty of an offence against this Act.

The aforesaid purpose included the smoking of cannabis.

The magistrates found that Miss Sweet had no knowledge whatever that the farmhouse was being used for such a purpose and she appealed, by case stated, to the Divisional Court, who upheld the conviction.

Miss Sweet further appealed to the House of Lords.

THE DECISION It was held by the House of Lords that in the absence of express words in the statute Parliament could not have intended the offence in section 5(b) to be one of absolute (strict) liability, thus the offence required a *mens rea* (mental element, literally a guilty mind). Since Miss Sweet had no *mens rea*, as she had no knowledge of the offence, the conviction was quashed.

COMMENTARY This case illustrates the application of the presumption that if a statute is silent about *mens rea*, absolute liability for a criminal offence cannot be imposed. As Lord Reid put it: '. . . there has for centuries been a presumption that Parliament did not intend to make criminals of persons who were in no way blameworthy in what they did. That means that, whenever a section is silent as to *mens rea*, there is a presumption that, in order to give effect to the will of Parliament, we must read in words appropriate to require *mens rea*.'

TAYLOR v CALDWELL
(1863) 122 ER 309

THE FACTS In May 1861 Taylor contracted with Caldwell for the hire of the Surrey Gardens and Music Hall on four days in the following June, July and August at a rent of £100 per day, for the purpose of a series of concerts. Between the date of the contract and the date of the first hiring the Music Hall was destroyed by an accidental fire, making the concert performances impossible.

Taylor, the hirer of the Music Hall, claimed compensation for the loss he had sustained due to Caldwell's inability to provide the Music Hall in accordance with the hire contract. The terms of the hire contract made no provision for liability in the event of the premises being destroyed before the hire dates.

THE DECISION The Queen's Bench Court held that looking at the contract of hire as a whole the parties contracted on the basis of the continued existence of the Music Hall at the time when the concerts were to be given; since its existence was something essential to the contract this became an implied term of the hire contract.

As the Music Hall ceased to exist without fault of either party both parties were to be excused from carrying out their promises. Thus Taylor was not liable for the agreed rent and Caldwell was not liable for failing to provide the Music Hall.

COMMENTARY This case on the frustration of a contract illustrates how unsatisfactory the common law was in relation to contracts that become impossible to perform (subsequent impossibility of performance) because of the principle that losses 'lay where they fell'.

Such situations are now covered by the Law Reform (Frustrated Contracts) Act 1943, which goes some way to remove the injustice of the common law.

However, consequential losses are not protected by the statute and so are often insured against.

THOMAS v THOMAS
(1842) 114 ER 330

THE FACTS In his will Mr Thomas made no provision for his wife but shortly before his death he expressed the wish that Mrs Thomas should continue to reside in his house for either the rest of her life or until such time as she remarried. After Mr Thomas died his executors entered into a written agreement with Mrs Thomas to convey the property to her for life providing that she remained a widow and paid the sum of £1 per year towards the ground rent on the property. Later the executors refused to convey the property to Mrs Thomas.

At first instance Mrs Thomas was awarded £100 damages against the executors, who appealed.

THE DECISION The sum of £1 per year to be paid by Mrs Thomas for the house might not be adequate consideration having regard to commercial letting values but it was sufficient consideration in law to support the agreement between the executors and Mrs Thomas.

COMMENTARY This case illustrates the principle in the law of contract that good consideration need not be adequate so long as it is sufficient in law.

It should be borne in mind that at the time of this case (1842) a married woman could not own money or property, etc., in her own name and that she was not protected by law should her husband die and leave her unprovided for.

VAN OPPEN v CLERK TO THE BEDFORD CHARITY TRUSTEES

[1989] 3 All ER 389

THE FACTS Simon Van Oppen, then aged 16, was a pupil at Bedford School and in November 1980 was badly injured whilst playing rugby football at the school. The plaintiff claimed the sum of £55,000 as compensation for his injuries from the trustees who were responsible for the running of the school. The sum of £55,000 was the amount that would have been paid under a personal accident insurance policy if such a policy had been in force to cover the plaintiff against the risk of injury whilst playing rugby at school.

In 1979 the Medical Officers of Schools Association issued a memorandum stating that due to the increase in serious injuries to schoolboys who played rugby, schools must take out accident insurance as a matter of urgency. This memorandum was received at Bedford School in July 1979 and the headmaster consulted the staff and some of the governors. It appears there was a division of opinion about the need for insurance and whether any insurance should be compulsory and obtained by the school or voluntary and obtained by the parents. The headmaster's letter to parents, sent out in December 1979, mentioned that compulsory accident insurance to cover injuries to pupils during any school activity (not only rugby) was being considered. The letter reminded parents that the school was not liable for purely accidental injury to pupils when negligence was not involved. Simon's father acknowledged that he must have received a copy of the letter from the headmaster.

The basis of the claim by the plaintiff was that Bedford School was negligent in either failing to take out a personal accident insurance to cover the risks of serious injury from playing rugby or, alternatively, in failing to advise parents of the risks of injury and the need for personal accident insurance. At first instance the claim was dismissed so the plaintiff appealed to the Court of Appeal.

THE DECISION It was held that a school was under no duty to:

VAN OPPEN v CLERK TO THE BEDFORD CHARITY TRUSTEES — *continued*

(a)   Warn parents of the risks of injury attached to playing games.

(b)   Advise parents to take out personal accident insurance to cover risk of their sons sustaining injury whilst playing games.

(c)   Take out any personal accident insurance for all or some of the pupils attending the school.

The claim for compensation was dismissed.

COMMENTARY   The decision of the Court of Appeal appears to be based on the school having no responsibility for any economic loss suffered by its pupils, which is the result of any failure to insure against a risk. The letter from the headmaster to parents may have been a significant factor.

Note: an accident insurance policy was taken out in 1981.

VICTORIA LAUNDRY (WINDSOR) LTD v NEWMAN INDUSTRIES LTD
[1949] 1 All ER 997

THE FACTS   The Victoria Laundry was unable to meet the demand for laundry services and could not take on large government dyeing contracts due to insufficient steam, so they sought a larger steam boiler. Newman Industries had a surplus steam boiler that was suitable, so they contracted to sell this boiler to Victoria Laundry, also undertaking to dismantle and to deliver the boiler on 5 June 1946.

Due to damage during dismantling the boiler was delivered 20 weeks late and Victoria Laundry sued for breach of contract claiming compensation for:

(a)   loss of profits from the laundry work they could not accept for the 20 weeks;
(b)   loss of profits from the government dyeing contracts they could not accept for the 20 weeks.

At first instance the Laundry was awarded only a small amount of damages, so they appealed.

THE DECISION   It was held by the Court of Appeal that the principle laid down in *Hadley* v *Baxendale* (p. 82) was to be applied, namely that the party in breach of contract is to be held liable only for the losses that a reasonable person could foresee as arising naturally, i.e., 'according to the ordinary course of things'. Losses arising otherwise are not the liability of the party at fault unless that party has special advance knowledge of the circumstances that would give rise to such losses. In the words of Asquith LJ, 'for a loss to be recoverable it must be 'on the cards' that such a loss would occur in the light of the knowledge of the party in breach of the contract'.

Newman Industries were liable for the loss of 20 weeks' laundry profits, but as they had no prior knowledge of the special dyeing contracts lost there was no liability for such losses.

COMMENTARY   The 'rules' in *Hadley* v *Baxendale* put a limitation on the principle that the award of money damages is to put, as far as is practicable, the injured party to the contract into the position he would have been in had the contract been performed.

THE 'WAGON MOUND'; OVERSEAS TANKSHIP (UK) LTD v MORTS DOCK & ENGINEERING CO.
[1961] 1 All ER 404

THE FACTS   A ship, the *Wagon Mound*, operated by Overseas Tankship (UK) was taking on fuel oil in Sydney harbour, when, due to the negligence of the crew, a large amount of oil was spilt into the harbour, where it drifted to a ship repair wharf owned by Morts Dock & Engineering Co. The fuel oil was set on fire by sparks from welding work in a ship under repair at the wharf, the resulting fire destroying the wharf. The New South Wales courts held the shipowners to be liable in negligence for the fire damage to the wharf, so they appealed to the Queen (at that time, the means of final appeal for legal disputes in New South Wales). The Queen referred the case to the Judicial Committee of the Privy Council, comprised of five Lords of Appeal in Ordinary, or 'Law Lords'.

THE DECISION   The Judicial Committee held that as the fire damage to the repair wharf was not a reasonably foreseeable consequence of the negligence by the crew of the *Wagon Mound*, the shipowners were not liable and the decision of the New South Wales courts be reversed.

COMMENTARY   This leading case establishes that the test of liability in negligence is based, *inter alia*, on the reasonable foreseeability of the damage happening as a result of the negligent act. As the then Lord Chancellor (Viscount Simmonds) put it: 'After the event even a fool is wise. But it is not the hindsight of a fool, it is the foresight of the reasonable man which alone determines responsibility.'

Students who wonder if oil on water can be expected to be set on fire easily should bear in mind that large amounts of oil leaked from the wreck of the *Torrey Canyon* at Land's End in 1967 could not be set on fire despite repeated attempts by the Royal Air Force.

WARNER BROS PICTURES v NELSON
[1937] 1 KB 209

THE FACTS The defendant, a film actress better known as Bette Davis, agreed to act exclusively for the plaintiff film company for a year and for no one else. During the year she contracted to act for another company.

THE DECISION The court granted an injunction to the plaintiff restraining the defendant from carrying out the contract with the other company.

COMMENTARY An injunction is an order of the court restraining a person from doing some act. It is an equitable remedy, i.e., a method of settling disputes which derives from that branch of law known as 'Equity'. The rules of Equity were developed in the former Court of Chancery and are still applicable today as 'a gloss on the common law'. They are based on what is equitable or fair; it follows that an injunction will only be granted where it is fair to do so having regard to all the circumstances of the case.

It will not be granted in a contract for personal services if its result would be to compel an employee to work for a particular employer or otherwise be redundant, e.g., if A agrees to give the whole of his time to the service of B and not to serve anybody else in any capacity whatever.

It will be granted to enforce a negative stipulation in a contract where damages would not be an adequate remedy. This case illustrates the point. The actress was not faced with the alternative of starvation or working for Warner Bros, since she had many other opportunities of earning a living.

Damages would not have been an adequate remedy, as it was the 'star quality' of this particular actress that Warner Bros required.

WARWICKSHIRE COUNTY COUNCIL v JOHNSON
[1993] 1 All ER 299

THE FACTS Mr Johnson was employed as the branch manager of the Stratford upon Avon branch of Dixons. He had placed a notice outside the shop stating, 'We will beat any TV, HiFi and video price by £20.00 on the spot'. Mr Thomas saw a television set offered for sale elsewhere in the area at a price of £159.95 and took Mr Johson to see it. Dixons had an identical set in stock so Mr Thomas sought to purchase it for £139.95. Mr Johnson refused to sell the set at the reduced price so Mr Thomas reported the matter to the trading standards department of Warwickshire County Council. They preferred an information against Mr Johnson under section 20(1) of the Consumer Protection Act 1987, alleging that Mr Johnson had 'in the course of a business of his' given to the customer a misleading indication as to price. The justices dismissed the information. The Council successfully appealed by way of case stated to the Divisional Court of the Queen's Bench Division, whereupon Mr Johnson appealed to the House of Lords.

THE DECISION Although the notice was deemed to be a continuing offer and misleading, Mr Johnson's appeal was allowed because the Consumer Protection Act was directed against employers rather than individual employees such as the manager of the shop, Mr Johnson.

COMMENTARY The decision involved an important point of law concerning the interpretation of statutes. In reaching their conclusion that the words 'in the course of any business of his' referred to employers, not employees, their Lordships had regard to what was said during the passage of the Consumer Protection Bill. The fact that they could do this was as a result of a judgment given not long before in the case of *Pepper (Inspector of Taxes) v Hart* [1993] 1 All ER 42. This important judgment permitted reference in strictly limited circumstances to statements made during Parliamentary debate on a Bill where such reference could help resolve ambiguity in the wording of the resulting

WARWICKSHIRE COUNTY COUNCIL v
JOHNSON — *continued*

legislation. Reference was therefore made to a reply given by the minister, Lord Beaverbrook, who said, 'I therefore think it is right so to draft the Bill that proceedings are directed against employers — that it is the corporate body standing behind the misleading price indication — rather than individual employees. Accordingly we have included the words "of his" in the Bill to ensure that individual employees will not be prosecuted'.

Clearly, then, their Lordships, in considering the case of Mr Johnson, had little option; as Lord Roskill observed, 'The adoption of the contrary construction woud be to reach a conclusion contrary to the plain intention of Parliament . . .'.

WELCH v CHEESMAN

(1974) 229 EG 99

THE FACTS   The plaintiff transferred ownership of her house (conveyed it) to the defendant for £300. She had lived with him for many years but only conveyed the house because he had threatened her with violence. The defendant died and the plaintiff asked to have the contract set aside. The house was worth about £3,000.

THE DECISION   The plaintiff was entitled to avoid the contract, which was entered into under duress.

COMMENTARY   Duress occurs when a contract is entered into as a result of:

(a)   actual or threatened physical violence or imprisonment;
(b)   threatened criminal proceedings.

The person threatened need not be the actual contracting party, but may be the husband or wife or near relative of the party.

A contract entered into under duress is voidable at the option of the party threatened, because consent to the making of the contract is not freely given.

When a contract is voidable it means that one party has a choice — he can either treat the contract as valid and binding or he can treat it as void. His option can be exercised without reference to the other party but in cases where property has changed hands — like the house in the above case — the court is called upon to 'set aside' the contract so that the property is restored to its original owner (Mrs Welch).

WHITE AND ANOTHER v JONES AND OTHERS
[1995] 1 All ER 691

THE FACTS In March 1986 the testator, who had quarrelled with the plaintiffs, his two daughters, executed a will cutting them out of his estate. In June the testator was reconciled with the plaintiffs and sent a letter to his solicitors giving instructions that a new will should be prepared to include gifts of £9,000 to each of the plaintiffs. The solicitors received the letter on 17 July but, due to various delays at the solicitors' office, no action was taken and the testator died on 14 September, before his wishes were put into effect. The plaintiffs brought an action against the solicitors for negligence. The court of first instance rejected the claim but the Court of Appeal held that the plaintiffs were each entitled to damages of £9,000.

The solicitors appealed to the House of Lords.

THE DECISION The House of Lords dismissed the appeal by a 3:2 majority. The assumption of responsibility by the solicitor towards his client should be held in law to be extended to the intended beneficiary who, as the solicitor could reasonably forsee, might, as a result of the solicitor's negligence, be deprived of his intended legacy.

COMMENTARY The plaintiffs had no contractural relationship with the solicitors so had to rely on the principles of negligence. For their claim to succeed they would need to establish that the defendants owed them a duty of care; this is a matter of forseeability. As Lord Browne-Wilkinson put it, 'If in such a case careless conduct can be forseen as likely to cause, and does in fact cause, damage to the plaintiff, that should be sufficient to found liability'. It therefore seems from the House of Lords' decision that once instructions are accepted to prepare a will for a client, a solicitor will owe a duty of care to his client (in contract and tort) and to the intended beneficiaries under the proposed will (in tort) to prepare the will with reasonable care, skill and expedition.

WILLIAMS v ROFFEY BROS & NICHOLLS LTD

(1990) 1 All ER 512

THE FACTS Roffey Bros & Nicholls contracted to renovate a block of 27 flats within a specified time-limit. The carpentry work was sub-contracted to Williams for the sum of £20,000. After Williams had carried out carpentry work on the main roof, completed work in nine of the flats and some work in the other 18 flats (for which he had been paid £16,200), he found himself in financial difficulties partly because the price he had quoted for all the carpentry work was too low. Roffey Bros & Nicholls became aware of Williams' difficulties and that the carpentry work had been underpriced. In order to ensure that the work was completed by the agreed time, Roffey Bros & Nicholls agreed to pay Williams an extra £10,300, at the rate of £575 per flat, as the carpentry in each flat was completed. Williams completed the carpentry work in a further eight flats and received a further payment of £1,500. Williams then stopped work on the remaining flats and brought an action claiming the sum of £10,847.

Roffey Bros & Nicholls denied they were liable to pay more than the original sub-contract price of £20,000, as the promise to pay an additional £10,300 was not enforceable since it was not supported by any consideration from Williams.

At first instance the judge awarded Williams a sum of £3,500 out of the extra £10,300 and Roffey Bros & Nicholls appealed to the Court of Appeal.

THE DECISION The Court of Appeal upheld the award to Williams of the £3,500 saying that the promise to pay the extra sum for the completion of the carpentry work was enforceable as it was supported by consideration. The consideration found by the Court of Appeal to be provided by Williams was the completion of the carpentry work on time thus enabling Roffey Bros & Nicholls to complete the main contract on time and avoid a penalty for late completion.

COMMENTARY This case develops still further the doctrine of consideration in the law of contract. The position can now be stated as:

WILLIAMS v ROFFEY BROS & NICHOLLS LTD — *continued*

Where one party to a contract agrees to make a payment to the other party over and above the contract price so as to ensure completion of that contract on time and thereby obtains some benefit, such as the avoidance of penalty for late completion that benefit can amount to good consideration for the payment of the additional sum. Even if no penalty is involved the avoiding of the need to engage a replacement contractor could amount to consideration.

WILSON v RICKETT, COCKRELL & CO. LTD
[1954] 1 QB 598

THE FACTS The plaintiff ordered a consignment of 'Coalite' from the defendants. Unknown to either party, the 'Coalite' delivered contained a detonator, which blew up in the plaintiff's fireplace causing considerable damage.

THE DECISION There had been a breach of section 14(2) of the Sale of Goods Act 1893. The goods supplied were not of merchantable quality because 'Coalite' accompanied by a detonator was not fit for burning.

COMMENTARY The defendants argued that there was nothing wrong with the 'Coalite' as such, and that it was only the presence of the explosive substance which made the goods dangerous. Lord Denning dismissed this argument saying:

> Coal is not bought by the lump. It is bought by the sack or by the hundredweight or by the ton. The consignment is delivered as a whole and must be considered as a whole, not in bits. A sack of coal which contains hidden in it a detonator, is not fit for burning and no sophistry should lead us to believe that it is fit.

Note: the Sale and Supply of Goods Act 1994, which came into effect on 3 January 1995, reforms the terminology of the Sale of Goods Act 1979 (formerly the Sale of Goods Act 1893). It replaces the expression 'merchantable quality' with 'satisfactory quality'. The change is intended to explain more clearly that the implied condition as to quality covers all aspects of the goods, including both aesthetic aspects (e.g., appearance and finish) and functional aspects (e.g., safety and durability).

WOOD AND ANOTHER v SMITH AND ANOTHER
The Times, 10 July 1990

THE FACTS   On 30 June 1978, a Mr Percy Winterbone made a valid will which had been prepared by solicitors. Two days before his death Mr Winterbone made another will, dated 18 April 1986. The later will was handwritten and duly witnessed by two persons one of whom pointed out that Mr Winterbone had not signed the will, to which the testator replied: 'yes I have, I have signed it at the top. It can be signed anywhere'.

The executors of the 1978 will sought to have the 1986 will declared invalid on the grounds that although signed and witnessed, the testator signed his will before making the disposition of his property. Consequently, the 1986 will did not meet the requirements of the Wills Act 1837, in that the testator did not by his signature intend to give effect to his will. (A signature on a blank will would not give effect to anything.)   The legatees under the 1986 will (Smith & Another) contended that it did not matter if the testator signed a blank will then had it witnessed and filled in the disposition of property afterwards, so long as it was all part of one transaction.

THE DECISION   It was held that the purpose of the requirement in the Wills Act 1837 was to reduce the risk of fraud. If a testator could say to the witnesses that he was about to make and sign his will, but would they witness his signature only on a blank sheet of paper, there would be no evidence from independent persons that they had appended their signatures to any disposition, notwithstanding that witnesses were not entitled to read the disposition. The executors of the 1978 will granted a pronouncement in favour of the 1978 will.

COMMENTARY   It is essential to bear in mind that although the testator can now sign his will anywhere, whereas formerly the signature had to be at the foot of the will, there *must* first be a disposition of the testator's property so that wherever the will is signed, it can be said that the signature is to give effect to the will.

USING CASES IN AN EXAMINATION

At the end of a GCSE Law course the student will have amassed details of a number of decided cases and may be wondering how to recall the case details under examination conditions. For most students there is no easy answer to the problem of recall; case details must be re-read as often as necessary. Self-testing is easily achieved by using the index to select cases at random to test recall.

But knowing a case is one thing; *knowing how to use it* is another. GCSE problem questions may or may not indicate the area of law involved and sudents must be prepared, if necessary, to identify the area of law with which the problem is concerned as a vital first step in preparing an answer.

EXAMPLES OF PROBLEM QUESTIONS

Where the area of law involved is NOT stated in the question

John sees a 'designer sweater' in a shop window with a price tag attached. The price tag reads 'SPECIAL OFFER—ONE ONLY @ £2.50'. Thinking he has found a bargain, John enters the shop and says he will buy the sweater marked at £2.50 in the window. The assistant, realising there has been an error, says that the sweater has been incorrectly priced and the correct price is £12.50.

John is legally entitled to the sweater at the marked price of £2.50.

This is a typical problem question on the law of contract, more specifically that part of contract law dealing with the formation of a contract known as 'invitation to treat'.

Two cases are applicable to this problem situation: *Fisher v Bell* (p. 74) and *Pharmaceutical Society of Great Britain v Boots Cash Chemists (Southern) Ltd* (p. 131). A reading of these cases will confirm the point at issue, namely that the display of goods in a shop, whether priced or not, is an invitation to treat and not an offer to sell; which means the prospective purchaser is invited to offer to buy the goods.

Students should not be misled by the fact that the price tag refers to it being a 'special *offer*'. This is a red herring — a trap to confuse the student with insufficient knowledge.

So, John is not accepting an offer, merely responding to an invitation to treat by making an offer to buy the sweater for £2.50. The assistant does not have to accept this offer and in this case (realising there has been an error) does not do so. Instead the assistant makes a new offer — John can have the sweater if he is prepared to accept the new offer price of £12.50. John can decline this new offer but cannot insist on having the sweater at £2.50.

Where the area of law involved IS stated in the question

Fred has his own road transport business and one day, while driving his lorry well within the speed limit, Fred knocks down and injures Bill, an elderly pedestrian, while Bill is attempting to cross the road.

Fred does not admit any liability, saying that Bill attempted to cross the road without looking to see if it was safe to do so. An independent witness of the accident says that Fred was looking at and shouting to another lorry driver at the time of the accident.

Advise Bill, who wishes to claim in the tort of negligence against Fred. How, if at all, would your advice to Bill differ if in fact Bill did not look to see if it was safe to cross the road before attempting to do so.

This is a typical question on the tort of negligence and although the examiner has indicated that is the main area of law involved, it is left to the student to see that contributory negligence is also involved in the problem.

Two cases are applicable to this problem situation: *Donoghue* v *Stevenson* (p. 67–8) and *Sayers* v *Harlow Urban District Council* (p. 184).

In *Donoghue* v *Stevenson* the House of Lords established the principle that every person has a legal duty of care not to do anything that can be reasonably foreseen as likely to injure a 'neighbour'. This means any person who could be so affected by the act, that the doer of that act ought to have such persons in his mind.

Applying this principle:

(a)   Does Fred owe a legal duty of care not to injure all other road users, including Bill?

(b)   Can Bill be considered a 'neighbour' in law to Fred?

(c) Is it reasonably foreseeable that a failure by a lorry driver to keep a continuous look-out for other road users may result in injury to them?

Affirmative answers indicate that Bill has a valid claim against Fred in negligence.

But if Bill contributed to the accident and thus to his injuries by not looking to see if it was safe to attempt to cross the road, this is contributory negligence and Bill's compensation will be reduced by the amount that the judge considers Bill was to blame. This principle was applied in the case of *Sayers* v *Harlow Urban District Council* and Mrs Sayers, who had contributed to her injuries, had her compensation reduced by 25%, the amount the judge considered that Mrs Sayers was to blame.

THE OVERALL APPROACH

To sum up, armed with the correct point of law and relevant case(s) the student should unite the two in his answer as follows:

(a) Identify the area of law concerned if it is necessary to do so.
(b) Explain the legal principle(s) involved.
(c) Support the answer with *relevant* case law, e.g., 'A case which illustrates this point is   v   , where the facts were . . . . ., and it was held that . . . . .'.
(d) Answer the *examiner's* question. In the examples given above:

> — Is John legally entitled to the sweater at the marked price of £2.50?
> — Has Bill a valid claim in negligence against Fred and how is that claim affected if Bill contributed to the accident?

It is not all that uncommon for examination candidates to forget the examiner's question in the heat of the moment and produce an answer to a question they have thought up!

Finally:

(a) It is generally better to avoid using the first person — 'I think that . . .'. Remember, it is legal principles that are being quoted, not your own opinions.

(b)   Always underline case names.

(c)   If the details of a case can be recalled but not the name of that case, say 'In a decided case where ...'. So long as the description of the facts/decision is recognisable the examiner will not usually deduct marks for the lack of a case name.

Notes

Notes

Notes

Notes

Notes

Notes

Notes

Notes